18. What does God do to the serpent who tempted the woman? (Genesis 3:14)

19. What is the woman's punishment? (Genesis 3:16)

20. What is the man's punishment? (Genesis 3:17-19)

21. What does God make for the man and the woman before sending them out of the garden? (Genesis 3:21)

DIMENSION TWO:
WHAT DOES THE BIBLE MEAN?

❑ *Genesis 1:1.* We can translate the opening sentence of the Bible in many different ways. The New International Version translates it, "In the beginning God created the heavens and the earth." Other translations attempt to show the dynamism of this act. *The New English Bible* translates, "In the beginning of creation, when God made heaven and earth." *Tanakh: The Holy Scriptures,* a new English edition published by the Jewish Publication Society, reads, "When God began to create the heaven and the earth." These translations show us that Creation is something dynamic. God introduces a process that begins with Creation.

❑ *Genesis 1:2.* The second verse shows us that God calls into being a swirling, watery chaos—lacking all order and capacity for sustaining life. The Hebrew word translated "the deep"* refers to this watery chaos that exists before God speaks and begins the process of establishing the creation as we know it.

❏ **Genesis 1:3.** The first act of Creation is the commanding word that light appear. This appearance of light, before God creates the sun, troubles many readers. The ancient Israelites distinguished between the light of day and the light of the sun. After all, they observed that on cloudy days, when the sun was not shining, light was still visible. So the sun was not the same thing as day, but was a characteristic of the daytime. The sun distinguished between day and night.

❏ **Genesis 1:5.** You may find it difficult to imagine God's making the whole creation in only six days. Through the centuries, many interpreters have thought that the length of the day at time of Creation was much longer than the twenty-four hours of our day. That thought seems highly improbable. The Hebrew writer was thinking of a day of the usual length, beginning at sunset and ending at sunset on the following day. The fact that God created the world in less than a week is one way of showing God's remarkable power.

❏ **Genesis 1:6-10.** The early Israelite and most of the people of the ancient Near East envisioned the world as an inverted bowl. This bowl separated the heavens from the earth and the underworld. The earth rested upon pillars that extended down into the deep waters below earth. This same firmament* or "expanse" kept the swirling waters in the heavens from flooding the earth.

❏ **Genesis 1:26.** The phrase, "Let us make man in our image" gives interpreters difficulty. Surely, God is not speaking of other gods who assist him in the Creation; that would be polytheism. Other commentators suggest that this phrase refers to the Trinity. Of the many explanations offered, the best one seems to be that God is surrounded by beings who do his bidding. They make up the divine assembly* in the heavens. We read about this divine assembly in Chapter 1 of Job and in Psalm 82.

❏ **Genesis 2:4.** Did you notice that Genesis 1 uses the general name *God*? But beginning with 2:4 the text speaks of *the* LORD *God*. These two terms, LORD and *God,* combine two ways of referring to God that we shall meet often in the Book of

4. What does God command the first creatures to do? (Genesis 1:22)

5. What position do the human beings occupy in creation? (Genesis 1:28)

6. After God creates the human beings on the sixth day, what does God think of creation? (Genesis 1:31)

Answer these questions by reading Genesis 2

7. What does God do to the seventh day? Why? (Genesis 2:3)

8. From what does God make the first man? How does God give the man life? (Genesis 2:7)

9. Where does God put the man? (Genesis 2:8)

10. What command does God give the man when God places him in the garden? What will happen if the man disobeys the command? (Genesis 2:16-17)

11. When God decides that it is not good for the man to be alone, what does God do first? (Genesis 2:18-19)

12. From what does God make the first woman? (Genesis 2:21-22)

13. According to God's instructions, what takes place when a man and woman unite? (Genesis 2:24)

Answer these questions by reading Genesis 3

14. What does the serpent tempt the woman to do? (Genesis 3:1-5)

15. What knowledge comes to the man and the woman when they eat the fruit? (Genesis 3:7)

16. When they hear the sound of God in the garden, what do they do? (Genesis 3:8)

17. Whom does God question first? (Genesis 3:9)

TABLE OF CONTENTS

1. Creation 2

2. Cain and Abel 10

3. The Flood. 17

4. Noah and His Descendants. 24

5. Abraham Settles in Canaan. 33

6. Abraham Speaks With God. 40

7. Abraham and His Descendants 48

8. Esau and Jacob 55

9. Jacob and Laban 62

10. Jacob in Canaan. 70

11. Joseph's Journey to Egypt. 78

12. Joseph and His Brothers. 86

13. Jacob and His Family Reunited 94

Glossary of Terms 102

Map: The Ancient Near East Before the Exodus . . . 112

*(Words denoted with a * in the text appear in the Glossary.)*

And God said, "Let there be light," and there was light (1:3).

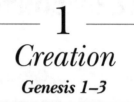

1

Creation

Genesis 1–3

DIMENSION ONE:
WHAT DOES THE BIBLE SAY?

Answer these questions by reading Genesis 1

1. Who creates the heavens and the earth? (Genesis 1:1)

2. What is the earth like when God begins creating? (Genesis 1:2)

3. What does God create on each of the first six days?

Day	*What God creates on this day*
One	(Genesis 1:3-5)
Two	(Genesis 1:6-8)
Three	(Genesis 1:9-13)
Four	(Genesis 1:14-19)
Five	(Genesis 1:20-23)
Six	(Genesis 1:24-27)

Genesis. The word translated "the Lord" is the ancient personal name for the deity, which is Hebrew is *Yahweh.** The other word is the general term for God, which in Hebrew is *Elohim.** A combination of the two is unusual, and it may point to two different traditions about the Creation that have been woven together. The combination *Yahweh Elohim* ("the LORD God") is not used after Genesis 3.

❑ *Genesis 2:8-14.* The word *Eden** means "delight" or "garden of God." In verses 10 through 14 the four rivers probably are the Nile,* the Tigris,* the Euphrates,* and (less certainly) the Ganges in India.

❑ *Genesis 2:20.* In ancient Israel, to name something defined and fixed its nature and character. Names expressed the essential features of that which was named. In giving the man the ability to name, God also gives the power to define and fix the very nature of these creatures of earth.

❑ *Genesis 3:24.* The cherubim* placed at the east of the garden to guard the tree of life were winged creatures that belonged to God's heavenly council. The word is plural. We do not know how many stood guard over Eden.

DIMENSION THREE: WHAT DOES THE BIBLE MEAN TO ME?

Dimension Three provides three major ideas that have meaning for our lives today.

Genesis 1:1–2:3—The Bible and Science

Relating the findings of science to the Creation story in Genesis puzzles many persons. Often persons too easily say either that Genesis 1 has nothing to do with science because it is a religious story, or that the story of Creation in the Bible contradicts the findings of modern science. Neither is quite right.

The Genesis story is good science for the time in which it was written. It explains how the world as we know it came into being at the bidding of a pre-existing reality. The Genesis story shows that everything in all the world draws its being from, and has its continued existence through, God's action. Scientific explanations of the development of life on our planet or within our solar system correspond fairly well with the biblical story.

The Genesis story is not in basic conflict with scientific theories because the Bible's account focuses on God's relationship to his creation. The story is one of fundamental religious significance, born in faith and nurtured in faith. Have you had difficulty reconciling the biblical account of Creation with scientific theories?

"God saw all that he had made, and it was very good" (Genesis 1:31). What does this sentence say about our world? What does it say about God's relationship to our world? What does it say about the people in our world? What does it say about you?

Genesis 2:14-17—Personal Relationship With God

As you read Genesis 2:4-17, you probably realized that this account of Creation differs from the one in Genesis 1. Many biblical scholars think the stories were written by two different persons or groups, each stressing particular features of the story of Creation. Perhaps a third group or individual combined the two stories. If this is the case, the present accounts of Creation found in the two chapters of Genesis give two important aspects of the Creation, each valuable in its own right. Genesis 1 tells the story in an orderly and measured way, giving great attention to detail. Genesis 2 gives us a more intimate picture of the first human pair and the ideal life they initially had with God in the garden.

But both stories are examples of sublime faith in the living God, the source and ground of life and its meaning. Both stories also place human beings at the center of God's concern and show that God lays a great responsibility upon the human community. We are to care for the whole of God's universe. The human being is responsible to God in a unique way. What insights into your personal relationship with God do you gain from Genesis 2:4-17 that you did not gain from Genesis 1–2:3?

Genesis 3—Original Sin

Genesis 3 tells how sin comes into the world. What is the sin of the woman and the man? The Hebrew text of Genesis 3:6 reads "she also gave some to her husband, who was with her." The serpent tempts the woman, and the man who stands with her is tempted at the same time and in the same way. Human history begins with temptation in this account. Genesis 3 does not explain the origin of sin. It does relate sin to realities outside us (the serpent), and also to realities within our minds and hearts. Sin arises from without us and from within us. It affects us all.

Many persons throughout the history of the Christian church believed that Adam's sin infected the whole of history thereafter. Does the Genesis story support this idea? If so, how does the sin of the first human pair affect later generations? How do we transmit sin?

The best explanation of the mystery of sin seems to be that every generation and every individual re-enacts the first sin. Each generation begins with the same gracious God that we see in Genesis 3. The story in Genesis 3 helps us see how sin is the free act of the first human pair, yet at the same time an act that has some of its origin outside the realm of human freedom. The mystery of sin is there, and where people are, sin is. Why do you think the writer of Genesis included this story? How do you interpret the story of Eden, of life in the garden?

Am I my brother's keeper? (4:9).

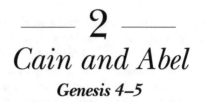

2
Cain and Abel
Genesis 4–5

DIMENSION ONE:
WHAT DOES THE BIBLE SAY?

Answer these questions by reading Genesis 4

1. What are the names of Adam and Eve's two sons? (Genesis 4:1-2)

2. What are the occupations of these two sons? (Genesis 4:2)

3. Whose sacrifice does God reject? (Genesis 4:5)

4. Who kills whom? (Genesis 4:8)

5. What does Cain say to God about his brother? (Genesis 4:9)

6. What does God do to Cain? (Genesis 4:11-12)

7. How does God protect Cain? (Genesis 4:15)

8. What is the name of Adam and Eve's third son? (Genesis 4:25)

Answer these questions by reading Genesis 5

9. How old is Adam when Seth is born? (Genesis 5:3)

10. Excluding Abel, who lives for the shortest number of years? (Genesis 5:23)

11. Who walks with God? (Genesis 5:22, 24)

12. Who is the oldest person to live before the Flood? (Genesis 5:27)

DIMENSION TWO:
WHAT DOES THE BIBLE MEAN?

❏ *Genesis 4:1.* The name Cain* in Hebrew resembles the verb *qanah* in sound. *Qanah* means to create or produce. However, this verse does more than explain that the Lord assists in the birth. The story of Cain's birth makes the point that the Lord intervenes to make this birth possible. At the time of birth, women often selected a name for the child that expressed their gratitude for God's gift of a child. This gratitude reflected in name choice was especially the case, when the parents finally conceived after a long period of barrenness.

In the second part of verse 1, the writer uses the name for God that the NIV (New International Version) translates as "the LORD." In ancient times the Hebrew word was *Yahweh.* In Exodus 3:13-15 and Exodus 6:28, God tells Moses this personal name. Moses is to use the name of Yahweh, or the LORD, in calling the Hebrews out of Egypt. Some scholars think that early Israelites told differing stories as to when Israel's God was first called by this personal name.

In Genesis 1, we find the general name for God—Elohim. Most of Chapters 2 and 3 combine the general name and the personal name. Genesis 4:1 uses the personal name alone for the first time as Eve* expresses her gratitude to God for allowing her to bring forth a son.

❏ *Genesis 4:3-7.* This brief story of the first sacrifices to God does not explain why either Cain or Abel* make sacrifices. They are not commanded to do so, but make a free offering of their goods to God. Abel is a shepherd, and thus he offers an animal from the flock. Cain is a farmer, and naturally he makes an offering from his crops. The background of this story of the first act of worship by human beings may be the conflict between the life of the farmer and the life of the shepherd. Cain and Abel are much more than individuals here. They stand for two ways of life—the life of the settled agriculturist and the life of the roaming shepherd.

❏ *Genesis 4:9.* "Am I my brother's keeper?" is an insolent statement by Cain that plays upon Abel's vocation as a shepherd. We might translate the expression to read, "Am I to shepherd the shepherd?"

❏ *Genesis 4:15.* We do not know what kind of mark God puts on Cain. It was probably a tribal mark to identify Cain as belonging to the Lord in some special way. Most importantly, this mark signifies God's protection of Cain from harm.

❏ *Genesis 4:17.* The Bible does not tell us where Cain finds a wife. This account indicates that God creates other families after the creation of Adam and Eve and the birth of Cain and Abel. Late Jewish and Christian traditions assumed that Adam and Eve had daughters, whom the sons married.

❏ *Genesis 4:17-26.* The genealogy* that appears at the end of Chapter 4 is quite similar to the longer genealogy in Chapter 5. These genealogies give us important information about the ancient Near Eastern world.* They do not talk simply about individuals, but about peoples—about divisions of time. The king lists* from the ancient Near East also divide the world into such lists. In these lists, the kings are said to have lived for staggeringly long periods of time. Some of these Mesopotamian lists show kings to have ruled for 72,000 years!

This genealogy follows the ancient pattern of identifying ten generations before the coming of the great Flood. For Genesis, those ten were (to fill out the list in Chapter 5): Adam,* Seth,* Enosh,* Kenan,* Mahalalel,* Jared,* Enoch,* Methuselah,* Methushael,* Lamech,* and Noah.* Several of the Mesopotamian lists give ten pre-Flood kings.

❏ *Genesis 5.* The long genealogies of Chapter 5 account for the entire period of time that elapses from the beginning of the creation until the Flood. If we count the year of Creation as year one, then the Flood begins in the year 1656, which is the year of the death of Methuselah. Noah is 600 years old when the Flood begins. He is the only ancestor listed in these genealogies of Genesis 4 and 5 who is still alive at the time of the Flood.

The two genealogies—one in Chapter 4 and one in Chapter 5—show that the writer had some knowledge of the ancient Near Eastern world. But the lists are certainly not simply borrowed from older Mesopotamian lists. These genealogies show the continuity from Adam and Eve through Cain and his wife. The sin of the first two generations marks the later generations, but they do their own sinning, as we will soon learn.

Of this entire list of ancestors who live before the Flood, only Enoch is faithful to the will of God—and Enoch lives for the shortest number of years! Enoch is an object of fascination in later tradition. The fact that he walks with God, and that God takes him (apparently without his dying) means that Enoch has a special opportunity to learn about the heavens, about the universe and its operations, and about life beyond the grave. Enoch is a central figure in much of the literature written between the Old Testament and the New Testament (from about 200 B.C. to A.D. 100).

DIMENSION THREE:
WHAT DOES THE BIBLE MEAN TO ME?

The story of Cain and Abel is tremendously important to our understanding of the Book of Genesis. The story is short, but its brevity claims our attention and forces us to ask questions. The events in Genesis 4–5 raise at least three issues that are relevant to our lives.

Genesis 4:1-7—Dealing With Rejection

Why didn't God accept Cain's offering? The story does not tell us. We could speculate that God considers the life of the shepherd more acceptable than that of the farmer. But why? Because of the sins committed by the pagan religions that were tied so closely to the natural fertility of the soil? Or because the wilderness with its simpler life offers a better prospect for people to remain faithful to God's demands?

Perhaps Cain does not offer his gift with a good heart and a willing spirit. Is Abel a just person and Cain unfaithful? If so, not a hint of such a moral judgment remains in the story. Maybe the story intends that Cain and Abel rectify their parents' mistake. The fruit of that tree was beautiful and good to eat. Eating the fruit offered the prospect of wisdom. Why, then, should they not eat it? The answer was that God said they should not. God's withholding the fruit of that tree from them did Adam and Eve no harm at all.

Just as not eating the fruit of the tree tested Adam and Eve's trust in God, so Cain and Abel's reaction to God's response to their sacrifices requires trust. After God rejects Cain's sacrifice, Cain could have sought God's guidance, without bitterness, and found out what was displeasing about his sacrifice. Instead, he becomes sour and embittered, unwilling to discuss the matter. God talks with him as a father talks to a son, reasoning the matter out, questioning Cain, waiting for Cain's response. Cain's scowl remains; he says nothing to God.

Everyone has experienced feelings of rejection from time to time. Think about the times you have felt rejected. How have you reacted to these feelings? Have you ever felt rejected by God? How did you respond?

Genesis 4:8—Premeditated Murder

The second issue that the story of Cain and Abel raises is whether Cain is guilty of premeditated murder. In the King James Version of the Bible, verse 8 reads as follows: "And Cain talked with Abel his brother: and it came to pass, when they were in the field, that Cain rose up against Abel his brother, and slew him." The translation of this same verse in the NIV seems to supply a missing sentence. This translation tells what Cain said to Abel: "Let's go out to the field." The first version implies that perhaps while they talk in the field, the subject of Cain's rejected sacrifice comes up. Perhaps as they converse about this matter, they begin to argue. Cain becomes furious and strikes his brother dead. This approach somewhat reduces the horror of Cain's deed. The NIV makes it clear that Cain deliberately plots his brother's death, inviting him into the field to attack and kill him.

It is impossible for us to be sure just which picture the ancient writer intended to give. Do you think that the story intends to present Cain as a murderer—or as a killer who did not plan his brother's death? How does the story come through to you?

Genesis 4:9-24—The Judgment and Grace of God

The story of Cain and Abel allows us to see both the judgment and the grace of God at work. Genesis 4:11-12 tells of God's curse of the ground in his judgment on Cain. The blood of Abel goes into the ground. Now the ground is damaged, wounded by human sin. It will no longer produce food for Cain. Moreover, Cain becomes a fugitive and a wanderer on earth, having no home, no land of his own, and no human companionship. He had a life with his brother, but he destroyed that life. Now he lives alone. Cain acted against the most essential element of the community—the family.

We also see evidence of God's grace in this story. After hearing God's judgment upon him, Cain objects, "My punishment is more than I can bear" (13). God responds to Cain's plea by providing protection for the first murderer. Cain will not die. God's mark singles out Cain as a person under God's care. God is with Cain from this time forward. God makes life possible even for the first taker of human life.

The story underscores the fact that human crimes cry out for attention, even before God intervenes. The blood of Cain's brother cries out, and God gives attention to that cry. As in Genesis 3, God comes immediately to the human scene when persons break their relationships with God and with one another.

In these early chapters of Genesis, the ancient writers show us that no time elapses between human failings and God's coming to address these failings. As we shall see in the case of the Flood, God does let some time pass, but the result is disastrous. Wickedness spreads to such an extent that humankind must be wiped off the face of the earth.

The first act of violence committed by one person against another ends in the death of one of them. But according to the Bible, God avoids the step that was almost inevitable in ancient times. God intervenes, and the killer is not subjected to the death penalty. Capital punishment is a burning issue today. Do you receive any help from this story in dealing with the question of taking the life of a human being?

Does your experience of God correspond to the judgment and grace we read about in Genesis 4? Do you think of God as one who both judges and forgives?

I am going to bring floodwaters on the earth to destroy all life under the heavens (6:17).

3

The Flood

Genesis 6–8

DIMENSION ONE: WHAT DOES THE BIBLE SAY?

Answer these questions by reading Genesis 6

1. Whom do the sons of God take as wives? (Genesis 6:1-2)

2. What is the length of life to which God restricts people? (Genesis 6:3)

3. For what is God sorry? (Genesis 6:6)

4. Who finds favor with God? (Genesis 6:8)

5. What are the names of Noah's three sons? (Genesis 6:10)

6. What does God decide to do about the sinful earth? (Genesis 6:13)

7. What does God tell Noah to build? (Genesis 6:14)

8. How does God plan to destroy the earth? (Genesis 6:17)

9. Who among human beings is to enter the ark and be saved? (Genesis 6:18)

10. How many of each kind of bird, animal, and "creature that moves along the ground" is Noah to take into the ark? (Genesis 6:19-20)

Answer these questions by reading Genesis 7

11. How many pairs of clean animals and how many pairs of unclean animals is Noah to take into the ark? (Genesis 7:2)

12. How long will the rain fall on the earth? (Genesis 7:4)

13. Who shuts the entire group into the ark? (Genesis 7:16)

14. How far above the high mountains does the water rise? (Genesis 7:20)

15. How long do the waters cover the earth? (Genesis 7:24)

Answer these questions by reading Genesis 8

16. As the waters recede where does the ark come to rest? (Genesis 8:4)

17. What bird does Noah send out first, and what happens to the bird? (Genesis 8:7)

18. Noah then sends out another bird three times, each time a week apart. What happens to this bird each time? (Genesis 8:8-12)

19. What does Noah do after he and his family and the animals leave the ark? (Genesis 8:20)

20. What does God promise regarding the future of the earth? (Genesis 8:21-22)

THE FLOOD   **19**

DIMENSION TWO:
WHAT DOES THE BIBLE MEAN?

❑ *Genesis 6:1-4.* This puzzling little story tells about a rebellion in the court of God that leads to the sin of angels with human beings. A longer version of this story exists in later Jewish literature (in the intertestamental* books of Jubilees and Enoch).

The story in Genesis says that the sons of God choose human wives, marry them, and have children. These children are called Nephilim,* which means "giants." We read again about these persons of great stature in Numbers 13:33.

Genesis 6:3 tells about God's decision to reduce the life span of all humankind. God's decision shows that God did not design human life to continue as long as it did for the descendants of Adam who lived before the Flood. Whereas Genesis 5 tells us that Adam's descendants lived hundreds of years, these verses in Genesis 6 say that from the time of God's decision, human beings will live for 120 years.

God's reducing the human life span to 120 years does not mean that everyone will live to be 120 years of age. Rarely do we hear of anyone living that long in our day. Rather, the story is saying that no one will exceed that age. God's decision applies to everyone except the patriarchs*—Abraham, Isaac, and Jacob.

❑ *Genesis 6:5.* God decides to bring the Flood because of the terrible wickedness on the earth. According to this verse, the source of this wickedness is with humankind. The language is sweeping: "every inclination of the thoughts of [human] heart[s] was only evil all the time." God's condemnation of humankind is absolute.

❑ *Genesis 6:14-22.* We can find flood stories similar to the biblical account in several ancient Near Eastern cultures. Each story has a hero like the biblical Noah. In the Gilgamesh Epic,* one of the best-known ancient Near Eastern stories, the hero's name is Utnapishtim.* The god Ea tells Utnapishtim about the coming flood. Utnapishtim secretly builds a large boat, launches it, and manages to escape with his family.

Our Old Testament setting is quite different. Noah does not build the ark secretly, but in full view of everyone. And he does his work at the direction of God. Noah, a righteous person, is unable to turn others from their evil. No one but his family joins him on the ark.

The dimensions of Noah's ark are approximately 450 by 75 feet, or 300 by 50 cubits.* It is 45 feet high, or 30 cubits. A cubit is the length of a forearm, from the elbow to the tip of the fingers—normally about 18 inches. The ark can accommodate the variety and numbers of animals, birds, and crawling things Noah will place in it.

❑ *Genesis 7.* In Genesis 7:2, we read that God instructs Noah to take seven pairs of all the clean animals and one pair of all the unclean animals onto the ark. God also tells Noah to take along seven pairs of every kind of bird. Previously in 6:19, we read that one pair of all the clean and unclean animals were to go into the ark with Noah and his family when the flood waters came.

This question about how many animals Noah places in the ark puzzles many persons. Does Noah take seven pairs of clean animals and one pair of unclean animals with him? Or does he take one pair of every kind of animal?

Our story is based on two different traditions. Scholars have found other, more subtle differences between these two early traditions. The message of Chapter 7 is clear despite the fact that different traditions are evident. The Flood comes at the clear direction of God, who reveals beforehand that a disaster is about to happen.

❑ *Genesis 8:4.* The mountains of Ararat* designate a mountain range in what is today the country of Turkey. Some expeditions to the modern Mount Ararat report sighting the remains of a wooden structure. However, the actual remains of Noah's ark probably no longer exist.

❑ *Genesis 8:6-12.* This beautiful part of the Flood story tells us how Noah knows when the waters have receded from the earth. In the Gilgamesh Epic, Utnapishtim also sends out a bird to see whether dry land exists. But the story of the dove—sent three times—that brings back an olive leaf in her beak, is a striking feature of the Genesis story. The dove has been a symbol of fertility, blessing, and peace from very early times.

❑ *Genesis 8:20-22.* The story tells us that God decides never again to destroy living beings or to curse the ground. In the new world after the Flood, the seasons will alternate at God's direction, and the ground will yield its produce. The animals, birds, creeping things, and human beings will be fruitful and fill the earth once more.

The story tells us that the sin of humankind is completely blotted out by the Flood. It also shows that the human sin the whole earth suffered is cleared away as the Flood cleanses the earth. Once the occupants of the ark take up their lives on earth, their prospects are much better because of this cleansing.

DIMENSION THREE:
WHAT DOES THE BIBLE MEAN TO ME?

The Flood story in Genesis 6–8 raises three issues that are relevant to our lives today.

Genesis 6:1-8—The Spread of Sin

In these verses, the Bible tells us how sin once again spreads in God's good earth. The heavenly host sin and interfere with life on earth, and humanity becomes corrupt.

God sees this wickedness on the earth and is grieved that he created humankind in the first place. Because of his sorrow at having placed human beings on the earth, God says, "I will wipe mankind, whom I have created, from the face of the earth—men and animals, and creatures that move along the ground, and birds of the air" (Verse 7).

Think about the times in your life or in the lives of others when one sin seemed to lead to another. How was this cycle broken? Was God's help required?

Genesis 8:20—Our Response to God

After the Flood is over, Noah celebrates his deliverance by building an altar and offering sacrifices to God. God also spares our lives through such acts of deliverance. Have you always recognized these acts of deliverance to be the result of

God's intervention? When you experience God's intervention in your life, do you respond by offering thanksgiving to God? What kinds of experiences in your life encourage you to commune with God?

Genesis 8:21-22—God's Forgiveness of Sin

Notice that the story in Genesis 6–8 does not name any victims of the Flood. God spares Noah and his wife and three sons and their wives—eight persons. From this tiny family God builds up life on earth once more. The Flood story gives us an example of God's drastic action to cleanse a polluted society. But the focus of attention is on the ark that carries human and nonhuman life to safety above the raging seas.

God remains committed to human beings and will not give up on them. Genesis 8:21 tells us that God will never again destroy every living creature by a flood. God promises to look after the human race and to order life in such a way as to keep open the possibilities for life on earth. God knows the character of humanity. God knows that we all have a bent toward evil. But God repeats his summons: "Be fruitful and increase in number" (Genesis 8:17). God recommissions humankind to care for the earth, to see to its needs, and to assist it in producing bounty for all living beings.

The story of Noah and the Flood portrays not only humankind's sin and God's judgment but also God's forgiveness of sin. How do you think God punishes us and our society for our sins today? How have you experienced God's forgiveness for your sins?

*I have set my rainbow in the clouds, and it will be the sign
of the covenant between me and the earth (9:13).*

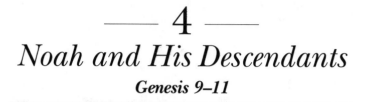

—— 4 ——
Noah and His Descendants
Genesis 9–11

DIMENSION ONE:
WHAT DOES THE BIBLE SAY?

Answer these questions by reading Genesis 9

1. After the Flood, what creatures live in fear and dread of humankind? (Genesis 9:2-3)

2. God allows persons to eat the flesh of animals on what condition? (Genesis 9:4)

3. When a person kills a human being, what is to happen to the killer? (Genesis 9:6)

4. With whom does God establish a covenant after the Flood? (Genesis 9:9-11)

5. What does God's covenant assure human beings about the world's future? (Genesis 9:11)

6. What is the sign of the covenant? (Genesis 9:12-17)

7. Who is Ham's son? (Genesis 9:18)

8. Who plants the first vineyard? (Genesis 9:20)

9. What happens to Noah when he drinks of the vine? (Genesis 9:21)

10. Who sees Noah in his drunkenness? (Genesis 9:22)

11. Who covers Noah? (Genesis 9:23)

12. Whom does Noah curse? (Genesis 9:25)

13. Whom does Noah bless? (Genesis 9:26-27)

14. At what age does Noah die? (Genesis 9:29)

Answer these questions by reading Genesis 10

15. Which son of Noah is the ancestor of the maritime peoples? (Genesis 10:1-5)

16. Which son of Noah is the ancestor of the Egyptians, the Cushites, and the Canaanites? (Genesis 10:6-20)

Answer these questions by reading Genesis 11

17. What do the wanderers in the land of Shinar first make? (Genesis 11:1-3)

18. What do they plan to build? (Genesis 11:4)

19. Why do they want to build these? (Genesis 11:4)

20. What does God do to prevent the people from continuing their work? (Genesis 11:7-9)

21. Who is the father of Abram? (Genesis 11:26)

22. Where does Abraham's family live? (Genesis 11:27-28)

23. Whom does Abram marry? (Genesis 11:29)

24. Do Abram and Sarai have children when they leave Ur? (Genesis 11:30)

25. Where do Terah, Abram, and other members of his family settle after they leave Ur of the Chaldeans? (Genesis 11:31)

DIMENSION TWO:
WHAT DOES THE BIBLE MEAN?

❑ *Genesis 9:1-7.* Genesis 9 relates the story of Noah's leaving the ark and settling upon the earth. The situation on the earth has changed remarkably. Fear and warfare have replaced the harmony that existed between humankind and the animals. Human beings can now kill animals for food. No distinction is made between clean and unclean animals, since this law is for all humanity and not for Israel alone.

Genesis 9:3-4 stipulates the conditions under which human beings may eat animals. In 9:3, God says that humans may eat any living and moving thing, as well as any green plant. However, Genesis 9:4 adds the stipulation that human beings must never eat the blood of an animal. In ancient Hebrew thought, the life of an animal is in its blood. One must not violate life, even that of an animal.

The most striking part of God's requirements of Noah is the way they protect human life. Putting these lines into today's language, we can read it as follows:

Those who shed the blood of mortals,
by mortals shall their blood be shed;
For in the very image of God did God make mortals.

In other words, Genesis 9:6 prohibits the taking of life. Why does God prohibit human beings from killing other human beings? The second half of the verse answers this question: because humankind is created in the image of God. The regulations God gives to Noah and his family show that although God has forgiven the sins of humankind, he is still taking an active role in the lives of his creatures.

❑ *Genesis 9:8-19.* Here we learn of an actual covenant* that God makes with the family of Noah and his descendants. Just as the regulations in Genesis 9:1-7 apply to all humankind, so the covenant between God and Noah is one that binds God to all peoples in all times.

The main content of the covenant between God and Noah is God's assurance that the creation is safe; it will not lapse into chaos again. God places the sign of his promise in the very structure of the creation; every time we see a rainbow*, we remember God's covenant. The sign is there for all to see, written in the skies. God is faithful, and we need not fear that our world will be swept away.

❑ *Genesis 9:20-29.* This story of Noah's curse on Canaan* is rather strange. The story's intention is to explain how the nations came to be separated into their present locations, and what their relationships to each other are. But the story also tells us something about the beginning of wine production, and what happens when Noah drinks too much of it.

In Genesis 5:29, we realize that Noah's name, given at birth, anticipates his discovery of the art of wine-making. The name *Noah* reminds the Hebrew writer of the verb that means "to settle down, rest, or find repose." For the ancient Israelites, the gift of wine-making was a very special and positive thing. Wine was refreshing and rest-giving, not something to be rejected. However, in this instance the consequences are regrettable, and the family protects the father from any shame connected with the event.

In this story, drunkenness has some adverse consequences. Ham* sees his father lying naked and reports it to his brothers. Shem* and Japheth* then cover their father carefully.

In verse 25, however, Noah curses Canaan, Ham's son, and not Ham. Possibly the story was once told about Canaan as the one who did the misdeed. Later on, the storyteller inserted Ham's name to show the evil of Ham's descendants. Many of the descendants of Ham were Egyptians, and the hostile feelings of the Israelites toward the Egyptians were great indeed.

The Canaanites were the real religious temptation to the Israelites. The attitude of Israel's leaders toward the fertility religion of the Canaanites and the loose sexual practices associated with such religion were probably the reasons for the curse of Canaan. Canaan, the grandson of Noah, here represents the Canaanite people.

The later application of this curse to black Africans, and the supposition that God cursed them and separated them from other people, is entirely false. This story does not support such an interpretation. Canaan is the ancestor of the Canaanites, who are a Semitic people and not black.

❑ *Genesis 10:1-32 and 11:10-32.* This long list of the family of nations contains information of great importance for the study of ancient history. The list shows the ancient Israelites' efforts to trace the family of humankind back to the first human pair and forward to the point at which peoples with their separate histories, languages, lands, and cultures cover the earth.

The Israelites use a different arrangement in noting the ages of the ancestors. The age of the person at the time of the birth of a son is first given, and then we learn how many years after that birth the father survives. To get the total age of these ancestors of Abraham, we add the two dates.

Shem, for example, is 100 years old when he becomes the father of Arphaxad.* He lives for another 500 years and has other children. His age at death is thus 600 years. This method of dating gives us a continuous chronology from the time of the Flood (which occurred two years before Shem became the father of Arphaxad, Genesis 11:10) on to the time of the birth of Abraham and his later call by God.

❑ *Genesis 11:1-9.* The story of the tower of Babel* is one of the most intriguing parts of this section of Genesis. The story begins by telling us that originally all of humankind had only one language. For some reason—we were not told why—these men and women began to wander eastward until they found what the Bible calls "a plain in Shinar,"* where they settle. *Shinar* is another word for the territory immediately surrounding the city of Babylon.

After settling, the people decide to build a tower up to the heavens in order to make a name for themselves. Most scholars believe that this tower refers to the great temple-tower, or *ziggurat,* * built in Babylon.* Babylonian ziggurats are stepped mounds made of clay bricks, with temples at the base and at the top. The ziggurat is the religious center of the city and serves as the meeting place of earth and heaven.

Seeing this tower as a symbol of humankind's ambition and desire for fame, God decides to take action. God confuses their language so that they cannot understand one another and scatters them across the face of the earth. The writer makes a play on the name of the city of Babylon (in Hebrew, *babel*) and the Hebrew verb *batal,* which means "to confuse."

DIMENSION THREE:
WHAT DOES THE BIBLE MEAN TO ME?

Genesis 9–11 raises four issues that have meaning for our lives today.

Genesis 9:1-7—The Taking of Life

Genesis 9:5-6 prohibits the taking of animal or human life casually. All beings who have the blood of life in them are under the protection of God. Persons are not to eat blood, and they are not to shed blood unless they are prepared to give an account of the killing to God. (See Genesis 9:5.)

The writer wants to show two things at once. Human beings may eat the flesh of animals; that is God's reward of grace. But as they do so, persons are to remember that animals also have life as a gift from God. Any careless or casual appropriation of that life for ourselves is not acceptable. Do you think that persons in so-called primitive societies treat animals better than we do? Do hunters normally respect and honor animal life in a proper way?

Genesis 9:20-29—Prejudice

Many persons believe that Noah's curse on Ham (through Canaan) justifies slavery and segregation. Remember the discussion in Dimension Two of the notion that Ham represents the black African peoples. The best way to respond to such misuse of the story is to point out that the curse is on Canaan, not on Ham, and that Canaan was not black at all!

For many persons, the word *prejudice* always means racial prejudice. What other kinds of prejudice can you think of? We all have prejudices; some are stronger than others. Are all prejudices misinformed prejudices? How can you help to remove the prejudices of others?

Genesis 11:1-9—Striving for Fame

The tower of Babel story in Genesis 11:1-9 questions our pride in our human achievements. Yet this story also reveals a longing for unity with God, for a life that reaches beyond the earth to the very gates of heaven. How does this story come through to you? Are the people building the city and the tower motivated only by pride and self-esteem, or are they also hungering for new ventures in community life?

Does the term *ambition* have positive or negative connotations for you? Have you ever felt that your ambition was in conflict with what God wanted you to do? If so, how have you handled these situations?

NOAH AND HIS DESCENDANTS   **31**

Genesis 11:1-31—The Mystery of God

The Bible gives no reason in Genesis 11:31 for Terah's* moving from Ur of the Chaldeans* to Haran.* The whole story of the beginnings of the Israelite people seems to leave God's choice of Abraham in mystery—as a decision that only God fully understands. How do you see the same mysterious movement of God in these first eleven chapters of Genesis? When has God worked mysteriously in your life?

Leave your country, your people and your father's household and go to the land I will show you (12:1).

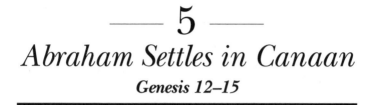

— 5 —
Abraham Settles in Canaan
Genesis 12–15

DIMENSION ONE:
WHAT DOES THE BIBLE SAY?

Answer these questions by reading Genesis 12

1. What does the Lord promise Abram? (Genesis 12:1-3)

2. Where does Abram stop first to build an altar in the land of Canaan? (Genesis 12:6-7)

3. Where does Abram next stop and build an altar? (Genesis 12:8)

4. What does Abram do when famine strikes the land? (Genesis 12:10)

5. What does Abram ask Sarai to tell the Egyptians about her relationship to him? (Genesis 12:13)

6. What does the Lord do to Pharaoh because of his taking Sarai? (Genesis 12:17)

7. What does Pharaoh do to Abram and his family and followers? (Genesis 12:20)

Answer these questions by reading Genesis 13

8. After leaving Egypt, where does Abram go in the land of Canaan? (Genesis 13:3-4)

9. What causes the trouble between Abram and Lot and their herdsmen? (Genesis 13:5-7)

10. How does Abram settle the trouble? (Genesis 13:8-11)

11. Where does Lot settle with his family? (Genesis 13:12)

12. Where does Abram go? (Genesis 13:18)

13. Where does the battle between the four kings of the east and the five kings of Palestine take place? (Genesis 14:3, 8)

14. What does Abram do when he learns that the four kings of the east have taken some of his family members captive? (Genesis 14:14-16)

15. What does Melchizedek, king of Salem, do? (Genesis 14:18-20)

16. What does Abram give Melchizedek? (Genesis 14:20)

Answer these questions by reading Genesis 15

17. Who does Abram intend to make his heir? (Genesis 15:2-3)

18. What does God promise Abram about this person and about the number of Abram's descendants? (Genesis 15:4-5)

19. What does Abram do with the animals and birds he brings at the Lord's command? (Genesis 15:9-10)

20. What passes between the animal pieces? (Genesis 15:17)

DIMENSION TWO:
WHAT DOES THE BIBLE MEAN?

❑ *Genesis 12:1*. The writer does not introduce the familiar name *Abraham** until Genesis 17. But the name *Abram** is simply a different way of spelling the same name. Names in the ancient world were often sentences that expressed praise or thanks to God at the birth of a child. Occasionally, a name expressed the parents' wish for the health of the child. The name *Abram*, or *Abraham*, means "may the (divine) father be exalted!"

The call to leave homeland and kindred was a much more demanding call in ancient times than it would be today. Abraham leaves the family and tribe that offers protection and assures his future to go into an unknown land at the call of God.

❑ *Genesis 12:2-3*. In ancient times, a blessing* was something very concrete. Words of blessing were more than a wish, or even a prayer. A blessing pronounced under the right circumstances could actually bring blessing. A well-known blessing is found in Genesis 27:27-29, where Isaac pronounces a blessing on Jacob.

❑ *Genesis 12:6*. Here we encounter Shechem* for the first time in the Bible. Shechem is Abraham's first stopping place after he enters the land of Canaan. Shechem was an important Canaanite city, which existed as early as 2000 B.C. Excavations indicate that Shechem was an important center for the people during the time of Abraham, Isaac, and Jacob. In Shechem, the early Hebrews entered into relations with the Canaanite population.

❑ *Genesis 12:7-9*. At Shechem, Abraham builds an altar and calls on the name of the Lord. The Book of Genesis shows the patriarchs moving about in the land, establishing friendly associations with the Canaanites. They build altars here and there, but they do not build towns or cities. The patriarchs are nomadic people—they are always on the move. They live in tents and only stop in certain localities to graze their flocks and perform simple acts of worship to the Lord.

❑ *Genesis 12:10.* Abraham's move to Egypt* when the famine comes should not surprise us. In the land of Canaan, just a small variation in the amount of rainfall brought catastrophe. People lived barely adequate lives and were subject to unbearable hardship if the rains were not normal. Records and paintings from ancient Egypt portray people coming into the delta region of Egypt to trade with the Egyptians and to settle among them for a time.

❑ *Genesis 12:11-15.* Abraham's telling Sarai* to present herself as his sister rather than his wife was not looked upon as an immoral act in ancient times. Travelers did what they could to protect themselves in strange lands, and such tricks were considered to be entirely all right.

The name *Sarai* means "princess," and princesses are by definition more beautiful than ordinary people. God later changes Sarai's name to Sarah* (in Genesis 17). Like Abram and Abraham, Sarai's two names are simply different spellings. Both names mean "princess."

❑ *Genesis 13:1.* This verse, as well as Genesis 12:9, shows Abraham to be wandering in the Negev* before he finally settles in Hebron. The Negev is the desert land in the southern part of Canaan. This somewhat hilly country was very heavily settled in some ancient periods of time and is heavily populated today.

❑ *Genesis 14.* Genesis 14 is a strange chapter. It does not resemble the other parts of the Abraham story, for it portrays Abraham as a warrior who is able to defeat the four kingdoms of the east. Nowhere else do we read about Abraham as a warrior. This chapter associates the patriarch with the king-priest of Salem,* Melchizedek.* We know from reading Psalm 76:2 that Salem is another name for the city of Jerusalem.*

❑ *Genesis 15:7-21.* These verses describe a mysterious ceremony associated with the making of covenants. Covenants in the ancient Near East are contracts between two tribes or two princes or two groups of people. The partners to the covenant here are God and Abraham. Abraham selects and dismembers the animals as a part of the covenant-making and the taking of oaths. Abraham is saying, "May what has happened to these animals also happen to me if I prove unfaithful to what I have sworn to do!"

The names *Hittite** and *Amorite** are traditional names that probably refer to two basic population groups in Canaan. One group includes those who moved out of the northern Arabian desert and settled in Mesopotamia,* Syria,* and Palestine. And the second group consists of certain Indo-European peoples who entered the area from the north and settled in with the general population.

DIMENSION THREE:
WHAT DOES THE BIBLE MEAN TO ME?

Genesis 12–15 raises two issues that are relevant for us today.

Genesis 12:1-3—God's Unconditional Love

Why did God choose Abraham to be the founder of the Israelite people? What reason does Genesis 12:1-3 give? It gives no reason at all. Notice also that Abraham does not speak a single word to God until God renews the covenant in Genesis 15.

The Book of Deuteronomy affirms that God did not choose Israel because of her great moral or religious virtues or accomplishments. God simply loved Israel and promised Abraham that his descendants would become the people of God in a special sense. (See Deuteronomy 7:6-9.)

Do you think that God loves us, his people, because of our virtues and accomplishments? Would God love us if we were not virtuous? Do you experience God's love as unconditional, as it was for Abraham?

Genesis 13:8-13—Trust in God

Abraham's readiness to let Lot choose any part of the land shows his generosity. It also shows that Abraham trusts the future of his people to God. It is true that, so far, God has not said to Abraham, "here is where you are to settle down and become a great people." But we who read the story know that Lot could choose the western lands, and Abraham would honor the choice. The richness and prosperity of the land to the east attracts Lot's attention, and thus the land of Canaan remains for the descendants of Abraham. Try to put yourself in the place of Abraham. Would you have trusted God to such an extent that you would have given Lot this same choice?

The theme of Abraham's trust in God is also present in Genesis 12:10. Abraham leaves the land of Canaan when the famine comes. But God sees to Abraham's needs, and Abraham returns from Egypt far richer than when he left. This danger to the land of promise is also the theme of Genesis 14, when the eastern kings threaten the land with their invasion.

We see in Genesis 13:8-13 and elsewhere in Genesis 12–15 that Abraham is a man who places his trust in God. He believes in the promise of God and is ready to follow divine guidance. Recall the times in your life when your trust in God has been put to the test and has held firm. What instances in your life have caused your trust in God to falter?

But Lot's wife looked back, and she became a pillar of salt (19:26).

—— 6 ——

Abraham Speaks With God

Genesis 16–19

DIMENSION ONE:
WHAT DOES THE BIBLE SAY?

Answer these questions by reading Genesis 16

1. Who arranges for Hagar to have Abram's child? (Genesis 16:2-3)

2. What is Hagar's attitude toward Sarai after Hagar becomes pregnant? (Genesis 16:4)

3. How does Sarai then treat Hagar, and what happens? (Genesis 16:6)

4. What does the angel promise Hagar? (Genesis 16:10-12)

5. What name does Abram give Hagar's son? (Genesis 16:15)

Answer these questions by reading Genesis 17

6. Why does God rename Abram? (Genesis 17:5)

7. From what age is circumcision to begin in accordance with the covenant? (Genesis 17:12)

8. What name does God give Sarai? (Genesis 17:15)

9. How old are Abraham and Sarah when God promises that they will have a child of their own? (Genesis 17:17)

10. What does God promise to Ishmael, the son of Hagar and Abraham? (Genesis 17:20)

11. How old are Ishmael and Abraham when they are circumcised? (Genesis 17:24-25)

Answer these questions by reading Genesis 18

12. Where is Abraham living when the Lord appears to him? (Genesis 18:1)

13. What does Abraham do for the three travelers who call on him? (Genesis 18:2-8)

14. What is the Lord's promise for Sarah? (Genesis 18:10)

15. What does Sarah do when she hears the promise? (Genesis 18:12)

16. What do Abraham and the Lord discuss? (Genesis 18:22-33)

Answer these questions by reading Genesis 19

17. Who meets the angels at the city gate in Sodom? (Genesis 19:1)

18. What does Lot do for the strangers? (Genesis 19:2-3)

19. What do the men of the city demand of Lot? (Genesis 19:5)

20. Whom does Lot offer to turn over to the men of the city in place of the strangers? (Genesis 19:8)

21. What happens to the men of the city as they try to force their way into Lot's house? (Genesis 19:9-11)

22. What do the strangers do for Lot and his family? (Genesis 19:12-23)

23. What happens to Lot's wife when she looks back at the burning city? (Genesis 19:26)

24. Why do the daughters of Lot choose to lie with their father? (Genesis 19:30-32)

DIMENSION TWO:
WHAT DOES THE BIBLE MEAN?

❏ *Genesis 16:1-6.* The practice of having children with the wife's maidservant was not uncommon in the ancient Near Eastern world. Inability to bear children was thought to be the fault of the woman. If a woman was unable to have children, she was considered a disgrace, a failure to her own family as well as to the husband and his family. In the ancient world, children were both an economic necessity and a mark of God's favor.

Sarah attributes her barrenness to the direct action of God: "The LORD has kept me from having children." Sarah's reproach of Abraham may seem strange, since she was the one who presented Hagar* to Abraham. Sarah wants Abraham to prevent Hagar from humiliating her. Abraham responds by allowing Sarah to treat Hagar as harshly as she wishes. As a result, Hagar flees into the wilderness.

ABRAHAM SPEAKS WITH GOD   **43**

❏ *Genesis 16:7-12.* An angel of the Lord finds Hagar by a spring of water in the wilderness. The story shows us a proud and self-sufficient Hagar who is unwilling to accept abuse from her mistress. Hagar is able to cope with her problems even though the time of her child's birth is near. God's angel persuades Hagar to return, after promising her a son whom she will name Ishmael.*

The description of Ishmael as "a wild donkey of a man" is probably not meant to be uncomplimentary. Ishmael will be somewhat like his mother: able to cope with any kind of situation, free and independent, living in the wilderness, and often at odds with his kinfolk.

❏ *Genesis 16:13-14.* The designation that Hagar gives to God, the "God who sees me," refers to the fact that God has seen her and promised Hagar and her child a future. If the New Revised Standard Version translation of the second phrase ("Have I really seen God and remained alive after seeing him?") is correct, Hagar is remarking about the fact that under normal circumstances, people who see God's face must die. In Exodus 33:20 God says, "You cannot see my face, for no one may see me and live" (NIV).

❏ *Genesis 17:3-5.* We mentioned in a previous lesson that the names Abram and Abraham are merely different ways of spelling the same name. Both names have the same meaning. In the changing of the names, the writer sees a change in the status of Abraham before God. Abraham's covenant with God is reaffirmed, and every time Abraham hears his name he will be reminded of that covenant and his special relationship to God.

❏ *Genesis 17:10-14.* These verses show that in ancient Israel, circumcision* served as a sign of membership in the community of the covenant. God instructs Abraham on how to insure that he and the members of his family are acceptable to God as a religious community. God makes this covenant with all males when they are eight days old. The covenant is marked by removal of the foreskin.

The health benefits of circumcision are well known, but the explanation given in Genesis has nothing to do with health.

Circumcision makes the person a member of God's people. It is a sign of divine action.

❑ *Genesis 17:15.* We noted in a previous lesson that like Abram and Abraham, the names Sarai and Sarah have the same meaning. Like Abraham, Sarah's status before God changes when God gives her a new name. Sarah now knows that she will bear the child for whom she has yearned for so long. God is responsible for opening Sarah's womb and allowing Isaac to be born.

❑ *Genesis 17:20.* Here we read that Ishmael, Hagar's son, receives God's blessing even though God rejects him in favor of Isaac. However, another major world religion reverses this picture. The prophet Mohammed taught that Ishmael was the true heir of Abraham. Therefore Islam is the true religion of the covenant between God (Allah) and his chosen people.

❑ *Genesis 18:4-8.* The meal that Abraham prepares is huge. He speaks about "preparing something to eat," yet prepares a massive banquet. The meal includes bread, a whole calf, curds, and milk. Abraham stands at attention, waiting at the table for these guests as they eat.

❑ *Genesis 18:11-15.* The reference to Sarah's laughing is the writer's way of bringing in the meaning of Isaac's name. A sentence such as "May the Lord give laughter" is possibly behind the name Isaac.* Here Sarah is laughing in her heart, and the Lord hears that doubting laughter and questions it.

❑ *Genesis 19:1.* The city gate* was the main meeting place in ancient cities. The gate area was normally quite large, suitable for settling cases of law. The gate area also encouraged social interchange and extension of hospitality. Lot* shows the same kind of hospitality to the travelers that his uncle, Abraham, showed.

❑ *Genesis 19:4-8.* The corrupt citizens who demand that the strangers be turned over to them for sexual abuse show that what God heard about the wickedness of Sodom* was true. (See Genesis 18:20-21.) A person's readiness to protect the stranger's welfare even at the expense of one's family is also a part of the law of hospitality in ancient societies. Lot's offering his daughters to the corrupt citizens of Sodom shows how much he honors his responsibilities as a host. But it does not speak well of his responsibilities to his family members.

❑ *Genesis 19:26.* Lot's wife turns into a pillar of salt because she looks back at the city. Several salt formations stand in the Dead Sea* region even today, and often one of these is pointed out as being "Lot's wife."

❑ *Genesis 19:30-38.* The story of incest between Lot's daughters and their father is not simply a scandal story about the origins of the people of Moab* and Ammon*—although that is part of the story's background. The story also shows the great demand for family and children in ancient Israel. Lot isolates his daughters and himself. The daughters apparently see no other alternative for any kind of life for themselves.

DIMENSION THREE: WHAT DOES THE BIBLE MEAN TO ME?

From our study of Genesis 16–19, we can see three theological issues that are relevant to our lives individually and as members of the Christian faith.

Genesis 16:1-7—Faith in God's Promises

The story of Abraham, Sarah, and Hagar is so true to human emotions and passions that we feel its truth and power. The conduct of the three is a revealing picture of just how people react in such situations. Abraham yields to Sarah and does not protect Hagar; Sarah goes too far in her jealousy of Hagar; Hagar lords it over her mistress.

Does the storyteller intend that we see Sarah's giving Hagar to Abraham as a sign of Sarah's lack of faith? Does Abraham's readiness to do so indicate his lack of faith? At what times in your life has your faith in God's promises faltered?

Genesis 17:9-14—Commitment to the Community

The unconditional membership in God's chosen people symbolized by circumcision is a striking truth today. Without participating at all in the religious traditions of Judaism, one may still find it impossible to escape the bond that unites a Jew with the Jewish community. That reality is visible in North America, Europe, and in many other lands—not only in the modern state of Israel. This reality does not center in circumcision as much as in being incorporated into the people of Israel, whether one wishes to be or not.

Do Christians experience this power of incorporation into the Christian community through baptism? Does baptism have such a meaning for Christians? What advantages does the Jewish community have in keeping a strong sense of community alive? What advantage does your baptism give to you as a Christian?

Genesis 18:22-33—The Mercy of God

Does the problem of destroying the righteous along with the wicked trouble you? Many Christians find the issue of God's governance of the universe very important in Christian theology. These verses do not settle the issue of how God is to give justice to all—punishing those who deserve punishment and sparing the righteous. The writer raises the question but does not answer it.

How much further do you think God would have gone, if Abraham had asked him to go further? Is there any limit to God's mercy when persons turn to God and plead with him in behalf of those who need his mercy? Would God withhold judgment if the number was no larger than five? or one? Would God have been merciful if no righteous persons were to be found in Sodom? What do you think is the limit to God's mercy?

*Take your son, your only son, Isaac, whom you love, and
. . . sacrifice him there as a burnt offering (22:2).*

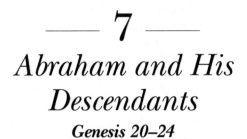

Abraham and His Descendants

Genesis 20–24

DIMENSION ONE:
WHAT DOES THE BIBLE SAY?

Answer these questions by reading Genesis 20

1. What does God say to Abimelech about Sarah? (Genesis 20:3)

2. Does God accept Abimelech's claim of innocence? (Genesis 20:6)

3. How does Abraham explain his presenting Sarah as his sister? (Genesis 20:11)

4. What has God done to the women of the house of Abimelech because Abimelech took Sarah? (Genesis 20:17-18)

Answer these questions by reading Genesis 21

5. What does Sarah ask Abraham to do with Hagar and her son? (Genesis 21:10)

6. How does trouble develop between Abimelech and Abraham? (Genesis 21:25)

7. What does Abraham name the place where he digs the well? (Genesis 21:31)

Answer these questions by reading Genesis 22

8. What does God command Abraham to do with his son Isaac? (Genesis 22:2)

9. Where does Abraham find the ram to offer as a burnt offering in place of his son? (Genesis 22:13)

10. What does God promise Abraham for not withholding Isaac? (Genesis 22:17-18)

Answer these questions by reading Genesis 23

11. How old is Sarah when she dies? (Genesis 23:1-2)

12. From whom does Abraham buy the cave of Machpelah as a burial place for Sarah? What is the purchase price? (Genesis 23:8-16)

Answer these questions by reading Genesis 24

13. What does Abraham make his servant swear not to do? (Genesis 24:3)

14. Who comes to the spring to get water as Abraham's servant waits and watches? (Genesis 24:15)

15. What does Rebekah do for Abraham's servant after she gives him water to drink? (Genesis 24:19-20)

16. What is the name of Rebekah's brother? (Genesis 24:29)

17. What does Abraham's servant do before he takes food from Laban? (Genesis 24:33)

18. What do Laban and his family ask Rebekah? (Genesis 24:58)

19. What does Rebekah do when she knows the man in the field is Isaac? (Genesis 24:65)

DIMENSION TWO:
WHAT DOES THE BIBLE MEAN?

❑ *Genesis 20:1.* We learn from reading this verse that Abraham travels to the city of Gerar.* Gerar is located south of the city of Gaza and west of the Dead Sea some distance into the wilderness region. (See the map on page 112.)

❑ *Genesis 20:1-18.* The incident between Abimelech* and Abraham closely parallels the one between Abraham and the pharaoh in Genesis 12. One intention of these stories is to glorify Sarah's beauty. They portray her as so desirable that she is immediately sought after by the king of the land. Later Jewish documents tell of Sarah's extraordinary beauty. One such document was found among the Dead Sea Scrolls and is called the Genesis Apocryphon.*

Abraham finds this wilderness area to have a sensitivity to morality that he had not expected. The inhabitants of Gerar were thought to be insensitive to fundamental human rights, and Abraham must be ready to protect Sarah from death even if he subjects her to humiliation.

❑ *Genesis 21:8-14.* This episode carries forward the story of Sarah, Hagar, Ishmael, and Isaac. Hagar's son, Ishmael, is playing with Isaac. Seeing them together reminds Sarah that Ishmael is Abraham's elder son. He might possibly claim the inheritance along with Isaac, or perhaps even in preference to Isaac. Sarah cannot permit such a thing to happen. So Sarah demands that Abraham dismiss Hagar and Ishmael from the household.

❑ *Genesis 21:27-31.* These verses tell how Beersheba* got its name. Because the Hebrew word *sheva* has two very different meanings, two explanations for the name Beersheba are behind this story of Abraham and Abimelech. One explanation told of a gift or pledge of seven ewe lambs made by Abraham as he and Abimelech sealed a covenant at the site of the well. Thus we have the name "well" (*beer* in Hebrew) "of the seven" (*sheva* in Hebrew). The other explanation is tied to the oath or covenant itself. Beersheba can also mean "well of the oath."

❑ *Genesis 22:1-2*. The story does not identify where Abraham is living when God calls him to offer his son as a human sacrifice. He probably lives at Hebron.* A journey from Hebron to Moriah,* which is in the region of Shechem, would have taken about three days. The distance is about forty-five miles as the crow flies.

❑ *Genesis 22:3-5*. The writer gives us many details about this important event in the life of Abraham. Abraham takes along the wood he will need for the sacrifice. He also takes fire, so that he can light a fire on top of the mountain. And he does not forget the knife. With these items beside him, he sleeps for two nights on the way to the land of Moriah, with his son sleeping next to him.

❑ *Genesis 22:9-14*. Just as Abraham is about to slay Isaac—at the last possible moment—an angel of the Lord calls from heaven and spares Isaac's life. Abraham sacrifices a ram whose horns are caught in the thicket. Then Abraham names the place "The LORD Will Provide."

Many scholars believe that the practice of offering the first-born son as a human sacrifice lay behind this story. But by the time of Abraham, it certainly was no longer the custom to offer human beings to the deity on a regular basis. Human sacrifice seems to have been an unusual act, done only on occasions of desperate need.

❑ *Genesis 23*. This detailed story reminds us of a transcript of a court proceeding. When Sarah dies, Abraham looks for a proper burial place. Burying the dead in caves was a common practice in the ancient Near East. The cave of Machpelah* was apparently near the center of the town of Hebron.

The story gives us a detailed account of how Abraham, with the greatest courtesy and generosity of spirit, deals with Ephron* the Hittite as he purchases the cave. He buys the field in which the cave is located as well as the cave. And he pays out the price that is asked—400 silver shekels. This amount of silver is quite a price for a cave.

The writer calls the people who live in Hebron *Hittites.* The Hittites were a small stratum of the population of Canaan, Indo-European in language and culture.

DIMENSION THREE:
WHAT DOES THE BIBLE MEAN TO ME?

These five chapters, Genesis 20–24, raise at least three issues that are relevant for our lives today.

Genesis 20:1-7—Dealing With Moral Dilemmas

Some readers think the story in Genesis 20 deliberately portrays Abraham as less sensitive to moral issues than Abimelech. We should remember that Abraham is the ancestor of the entire people of Israel. He must stay alive until he and Sarah have a child. Thus the story portrays Abraham as fearful for his own life and ready to expose Sarah to danger and even death.

Think about the times in your life when you have found yourself in moral dilemmas. Have you ever had to endanger family or loved ones for what you perceived to be a good reason? Because of Abimelech's integrity and the guidance of God, Abraham's deception turned out for the best. Have you felt God's presence when facing moral crises? Did these situations turn out for the best?

Genesis 22:1-14—Testing Our Faith in God

The story of Abraham's offering of Isaac is a classic picture of Abraham's faith. It is told with a power and beauty that are almost overwhelming. God knows what a test of faith Abraham will experience. We also know that it is a test, but Abraham believes that God's demand may stand. He has to prepare himself for the possibility that God is not merely testing him. And the details of the story show that Abraham does so.

What must Abraham have thought when he heard God's demand? Isaac represents God's promise to Abraham of many descendants. Abraham and Sarah had waited many years for

Isaac. What God wants is Abraham's complete commitment in faith.

We have all been through times in our lives when our faith in God has been put to the test. God requires things of us that we find difficult to do. In these situations in your life, did you respond as Abraham did?

This story of Isaac's near-sacrifice is immensely important in later Jewish and Christian thought. What parallels do you see between Abraham's offering of Isaac and Christ's offering of himself?

Genesis 24:52-61—Courage to Face the Unknown

In this story of Isaac's marriage to Rebekah,* Abraham's servant arranges for the wedding before Rebekah meets Isaac. After the arrangements are made between the servant and Rebekah's family, her father and brother ask that she be allowed to remain with them for ten days. Abraham's servant states his preference that she return with him immediately.

Bethuel* and Laban* call Rebekah and ask her, "Will you go with this man?" She says, "I will go." Imagine how Rebekah must have felt. She agrees unhesitatingly to go with a man she does not know, to a territory that is unfamiliar to her, to marry a man she has never seen. Would you have the courage to give Rebekah's answer? How have you faced the unknown aspects of the future in your life?

*The voice is the voice of Jacob, but the hands are the
hands of Esau (27:22).*

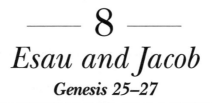

— 8 —
Esau and Jacob
Genesis 25–27

DIMENSION ONE:
WHAT DOES THE BIBLE SAY?

Answer these questions by reading Genesis 25

1. Whom does Abraham take as a wife? (Genesis 25:1)

2. How old is Abraham when he dies? (Genesis 25:7)

3. Where do his sons bury him? (Genesis 25:9)

4. To which of the twin sons does Rebekah give birth first?
   (Genesis 25:25-26)

5. Which son does each parent favor? (Genesis 25:28)

6. What does Esau give Jacob in exchange for some lentil stew and bread? (Genesis 25:29-34)

Answer these questions by reading Genesis 26

7. How does Isaac identify Rebekah to the people of Gerar? (Genesis 26:7)

8. What creates tension between the people of Gerar and Isaac's people? (Genesis 26:17-22)

Answer these questions by reading Genesis 27

9. Whom does Isaac ask to prepare special food for him as he draws near to death? (Genesis 27:1-4)

10. Who actually prepares the food, and who brings it to Isaac? (Genesis 27:6-10)

11. How does Jacob disguise himself as Esau? (Genesis 27:15-16)

12. What does Isaac's blessing include? (Genesis 27:28-29)

13. When Esau brings food for Isaac, what does Isaac do? (Genesis 27:30-33)

14. What is Isaac's blessing upon Esau? (Genesis 27:39-40)

15. What does Rebekah advise Jacob to do in order to escape harm at the hands of Esau? (Genesis 27:43-45)

DIMENSION TWO:
WHAT DOES THE BIBLE MEAN?

❏ *Genesis 25:1-6.* This genealogy of Abraham's wife Keturah* links Abraham and his descendants with certain Arabian tribes of the northern desert. Abraham takes Keturah as his wife so that he can have the very large family that was highly prized in the ancient world. However, Keturah is not a link in the genealogy of the divine promise; the story makes this clear. Abraham gives generous gifts to this part of his family and sends them to the eastern desert region to live. Abraham reserves his entire inheritance for Isaac.

❏ *Genesis 25:7-11.* Notice that both Isaac and Ishmael bury their father Abraham in the cave of Machpelah. Although he does not share in Abraham's inheritance, Ishmael is fully entitled to share in the act of burying his father. It is essential for a son to take part in laying his father to rest. We also learn in these verses that God's blessing follows Isaac, not Ishmael.

❏ *Genesis 25:21-23.* The story of the birth of Jacob* and Esau* contains a number of familiar themes. Again and again in the Bible, the women who bear children of great importance are at first unable to have children at all. God's blessing finally favors them, and the parents and the community recognize the child or children as all the more given by God.

❑ *Genesis 25:24-26.* The identification of Esau as a child with a ruddy complexion probably is a play on the word *Edom,** which means "red." The country of Edom contains some beautiful rose-red mountains, the most spectacular of which are found in modern Petra in Jordan. In a later lesson we will see that Esau is traditionally thought of as the father of the Edomites.

Esau is also a hairy child. This fact prepares us for the later story of how Jacob manages to deceive Isaac into believing that Jacob is the hairy Esau.

Jacob's taking hold of Esau's heel shows how Jacob, even before birth, tries to get the better of his brother Esau. It probably also shows that Jacob is a fighter, a tenacious struggler for life and blessing. Jacob's name means "the supplanter," or the one who takes the place of another.

❑ *Genesis 25:27-28.* Jacob is a tent-dwelling shepherd. But Esau delights in hunting and in feasting on his catch. The writer presents Esau as a rough and perhaps unthinking person. On the other hand, we see Jacob as reflective, ambitious, and shrewd. Esau and his father Isaac care for each other in a special way, and Jacob and Rebekah are particularly close.

❑ *Genesis 25:29-34.* We do not know exactly how a father passed along the birthright* to the eldest, or the favorite, son. A double portion of the family goods probably went to the eldest son, who became the head of the household at the father's death. Or perhaps specific property was committed to the eldest son during the father's lifetime, property that the son would inherit on the father's death.

The clever Jacob, taking advantage of Esau's unlimited appetite, makes Esau swear to pass on his birthright to Jacob in exchange for a meal. An oath, of course, has binding authority that a mere promise from Esau would not have. The story clearly criticizes Esau more than Jacob, for Esau's interest lies in filling his belly rather than upholding the name and honor of his father Isaac and his grandfather Abraham.

❑ *Genesis 26:1-5.* The events in Isaac's life are much like those in Abraham's. Abraham encountered a famine (Genesis 12) and went to Egypt to escape it, thereby endangering his life and the promise. Isaac also faces famine, but God tells him not to go to Egypt. God promises Isaac great blessings if he will remain in the land and place his trust in God. Isaac's connection with Gerar is like that of Abraham, which we noted in Genesis 20.

❏ *Genesis 26:5-11.* For the third time, a patriarch presents his wife as his sister. (See Genesis 12 and Genesis 20.) On this occasion, however, no one takes Rebekah into his household. But Isaac's act endangers her life and honor. Abimelech scolds Isaac for his lie after he accidentally discovers that Isaac and Rebekah are husband and wife.

Abimelech lives in a house in the city of Gerar. Isaac and Rebekah live nearby, close enough for Abimelech to see them from his window. Abimelech sees Isaac fondling Rebekah and realizes that they are not brother and sister. The Hebrew word translated "fondling" is akin to the name *Isaac,* so we have a word play in this story.

❏ *Genesis 26:34-35.* Since Esau is the ancestor of the Edomites, it is difficult to understand why he marries a Hittite woman. Probably the term *Hittite* simply refers to the inhabitants of the land who were not part of Abraham and Isaac's family, and thus unsuitable marriage partners for Esau. Just as Esau despised his birthright, he also despises his family ancestry. The genealogy here does not entirely agree with the fuller one found in Genesis 36.

❏ *Genesis 27:1-4.* The story in Chapter 27 has a single theme from beginning to end: Isaac's last blessing upon his sons. Here we read that Jacob receives the blessing in place of Esau. In the ancient world, the time of death was a time when the powers of the dying head of the family could be rallied to enable him to pronounce his last will and testament in the form of a blessing.

The blessing on this occasion supposedly stemmed from a special gift of seeing into the future, possibly only at the moment of death. The act of blessing in words of poetry set the blessing into motion and brought about what was pronounced. Once these power-laden words of blessing were spoken, they could not be recalled.

Sometimes food contributed to the power and effectiveness of the blessing. That is why Isaac makes so much of Esau's securing and preparing a special meal, for Esau is to receive

ESAU AND JACOB

the greater blessing. The ancient Israelites understood the blessing to be very much under the control of God.

❑ *Genesis 27:39-40.* The blessing that falls on Esau is more of a curse than a blessing. But it does refer to a time when Esau will break loose and come to freedom. In fact, the people of Edom, who are the descendants of Esau, become a very powerful kingdom indeed. The Idumeans* are their later descendants. Herod the Great, an Idumean, becomes king over the Jews just before the time of Jesus' ministry.

DIMENSION THREE:
WHAT DOES THE BIBLE MEAN TO ME?

Genesis 25–27 provides us with three issues that are relevant for our lives today.

Genesis 25:1-6—Polygamy

In ancient Israel, having more than one wife was not a problem. Abraham's marriages to Sarah and Keturah were considered regular marriages. In later history however, the multiple marriages of Abraham and the other patriarchs caused trouble for the Jewish and Christian communities.

Persons often point out that polygamy usually is practiced in societies where the infant mortality rate is high, and where warfare decimates the male population. In Abraham's society, having many descendants was thought to be a sign of God's favor. Do you think Abraham's polygamy is justified under these circumstances? How can you justify the practice of polygamy today?

Genesis 25:29-34—The Importance of Family

The Bible condemns Esau's contempt of his birthright, but it does not condemn Jacob's taking advantage of Esau's hunger. Does the story consider Jacob's winning away Esau's birthright as an immoral act? The fact that Esau despises his birthright tells us that Esau has little regard for his family. Think about the times when your family members have disappointed you. Have you ever been tempted to renounce your family ties? What reasons would cause you to take such a drastic step? Can you understand how Esau could have done such a thing?

Genesis 27:1-29—Living With Deceit

What do we say about Jacob's deception of his blind father Isaac? Surely the story intends to show that Jacob and Rebekah went too far in stealing away the blessing of Isaac. Esau in this case does what his father asks him to do, and he still loses the blessing. But we know that Esau cared little about his family relationship. Would it have been disastrous for Esau to receive the blessing? Would Esau have cared anything about the promise made to Abraham and confirmed to Isaac?

Can you think of times when deceit is acceptable? We all have deceived others at one time or another. Looking back on these situations in your life, do you think now that you did the right thing? How do you justify these situations in your life and the lives of others?

May the LORD keep watch between you and me when we are away from each other (31:49).

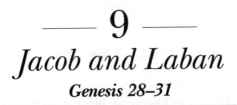

9

Jacob and Laban

Genesis 28–31

DIMENSION ONE: WHAT DOES THE BIBLE SAY?

Answer these questions by reading Genesis 28

1. Where does Isaac send Jacob to find a wife for himself from his own family? (Genesis 28:1-2)

2. What does Esau do when he hears that Isaac will not let Jacob marry one of the Canaanite women? (Genesis 28:8-9)

3. What does Jacob name the place where he has the dream? (Genesis 28:19)

4. What does Jacob promise to give to God if God blesses him on his journey? (Genesis 28:22)

Answer these questions by reading Genesis 29

5. Where does Jacob meet Rachel? (Genesis 29:2-9)

6. After Jacob serves seven years for Laban's daughter Rachel, whom does Laban give him to marry? (Genesis 29:23-25)

7. How long does Jacob wait before he receives Rachel as his wife? (Genesis 29:27-28)

8. How many additional years does Jacob serve Laban in payment for Rachel? (Genesis 29:30)

9. Which of Jacob's two wives has the first child? (Genesis 29:31-32)

10. What are the names of Leah's first four children? (Genesis 29:32-35)

Answer these questions by reading Genesis 30

11. What are the names of the sons born to Rachel's servant Bilhah? (Genesis 30:6-8)

12. What are the names of the sons born to Jacob and Zilpah, the servant of Leah? (Genesis 30:9-13)

13. What are the names of the additional two sons born to Leah and Jacob? (Genesis 30:18-20)

14. What is the name of the daughter born to Leah and Jacob? (Genesis 30:21)

15. What is the name of Rachel's first son? (Genesis 30:24)

16. How does Laban attempt to cheat Jacob after Laban agrees to the distribution of the flocks? (Genesis 30:35-36)

Answer these questions by reading Genesis 31

17. Why do Leah and Rachel agree to return to Canaan with Jacob? (Genesis 31:14-16)

18. What does Rachel steal from her father before she leaves with Jacob? (Genesis 31:19)

19. What does Laban do when he hears that Jacob has left for Canaan? (Genesis 31:22-23)

20. What does the covenant between Laban and Jacob guarantee each of them? (Genesis 31:49-52)

DIMENSION TWO:
WHAT DOES THE BIBLE MEAN?

❏ *Genesis 28:1.* We learned in the previous lesson that Rebekah says she cannot endure Jacob's marrying one of the Hittite women (Genesis 27:46). In Genesis 28:1 Jacob calls these same women Canaanites. *Canaanite* is the more general term for the inhabitants of the land.

❏ *Genesis 28:10-22.* Jacob leaves Beersheba and travels toward Haran. Haran is located on the western end of the Euphrates River, so Jacob was traveling north.

The place where Jacob has his dream is probably the same place where Abraham built an altar to the Lord (Genesis 12:8) between Bethel* and Ai.* The name *Bethel* means "the house of God." Jacob's reference to "the gate of heaven" probably arises from the belief that the mountaintop places of worship were places where the heavens and the earth met. They were the entryways to the realm of the gods.

As Jacob leaves the land where he is known and has protection, he needs the protection of God. Thus he makes his vow. He promises to give one-tenth of all his goods to God upon his safe return, if God will provide for his needs and protect him. This story is one source for the payment of a tenth, or a tithe,* to God.

❏ *Genesis 29:1.* This verse tells us that Jacob travels to the land of the "eastern people."* This very general expression refers to the Arabian neighbors of the Israelites.

❏ *Genesis 29:7-8.* Jacob cannot understand why the shepherds are not watering their flocks. What do the shepherds mean when they tell Jacob they cannot water the sheep until all the flocks are gathered, and the stone is rolled away? The story does not answer this question, but two reasons are possible. Since all the shepherds have equal rights to the water, the custom was to remove the stone only when all parties were present. Thus no shepherd could accuse another of deceit.

This story of Jacob at the well draws on an ancient picture of Jacob as an enormously strong person. Jacob single-handedly removes the stone slab that covers the well. We can imagine that normally the stone could only be removed when several male shepherds gather at the well and join forces to move it.

❏ *Genesis 29:16-17.* The reference to Leah's* weak eyes apparently means that she lacks the beauty of her younger sister Rachel.* Her eyes are pale and dull, not bright.

❏ *Genesis 29:21-23.* Ancient marriage custom would allow Laban to substitute Leah for Rachel. But modern readers may wonder how Jacob could have been deceived into thinking that Leah was Rachel. The writer of this story assumes that his audience knows about the ancient custom of veiling the bride on her wedding night. After being heavily veiled, the bride was presented to the bridegroom after darkness had fallen. Thus it is not surprising that Jacob discovers the trick Laban played on him only when the morning came.

❏ *Genesis 29:31-35.* One of the touching points in this story is the writer's relating Leah's not being the favored wife to the fact of her bearing so many sons. Because Jacob hates her, God gives her sons in compensation. The names Leah gives to her three sons (Reuben,* Simeon,* and Levi*) all have special meanings for Leah.

❏ *Genesis 30:1-13.* Like Sarah before her, Rachel despairs of having children of her own. She gives her servant, Bilhah*, to her husband to bear her children. In Rachel's mind, this action is equivalent to having born Dan* and Naphtali* herself. Leah also bears Gad* and Asher* through her servant Zilpah.* The practice of women having children through their servants is known in other parts of the ancient Near East. We encountered a similar situation with Sarah and Hagar in Genesis 16.

❏ *Genesis 30:14-16.* The mandrake* is a plant that the ancient world used to promote fertility. Its fruit resembles a plum. The fact that Rachel is the loved wife is underscored by this story of the mandrakes that Reuben gives to his mother Leah. Rachel can count on the loving companionship of her husband Jacob; Leah has to resort to all kinds of strategies to get her husband's attention. Rachel thus agrees to a fair exchange. She gets the mandrakes to remove her barrenness, and Leah gets some of Jacob's attention.

❏ *Genesis 30:17-24.* In these verses we read about Leah's fourth and fifth sons, Issachar* and Zebulun.* God opens Rachel's womb, and she has a son whom she names Joseph.* Again, Leah and Rachel offer explanations for the names of their sons.

❏ *Genesis 31:1-5.* Jacob gives several reasons for deciding to return to his homeland. The first reason is the growing hostility between Jacob and the sons of Laban. Second, the Lord comes to Jacob in a dream and orders him to return. Third, Laban himself no longer regards Jacob with favor. Possibly Laban has decided that he cannot outdo Jacob in cleverness and had better be rid of this shepherd.

❏ *Genesis 31:14-16.* The two daughters of Laban realize that they will receive no inheritance from their father. We know that daughters could inherit the estate of their father when there were no male descendants in the family. But Laban regards his own daughters as foreigners. They believe that the wiser course of action is to go with Jacob, since all their goods will go with him.

❏ *Genesis 31:43-50.* The covenant that Jacob and Laban make in Gilead* is designed to keep the two rivals in their respective places. You may be familiar with the Mizpah benediction,* "May the LORD keep watch between you and me when we are away from each other." This benediction is often used in Christian youth groups and is based on the words of the covenant between Jacob and Laban. Its original meaning was something like, "May the Lord keep his eye on both of us and prevent us from doing mischief to the other person when the opportunity comes!"

DIMENSION THREE:
WHAT DOES THE BIBLE MEAN TO ME?

In the third dimension you will discuss how the Scripture is relevant for your life today. Genesis 28–31 provides four issues for this discussion.

Genesis 28:12-17—Receiving God's Blessings

The Lord's blessing on Jacob is similar to God's blessing of Abraham. Refresh your memory by reading Genesis 12:1-3. God's blessing on Jacob is more explicit, probably because Jacob will face danger outside the land of promise.

Apparently, the dream of the ladder connecting earth and heaven, with angels ascending and descending, makes Jacob fearful. Perhaps he now recognizes Bethel as an immensely holy place—the very meeting place of earth and heaven.

Whatever Jacob's reason, the important thing to remember is that Jacob reacts fearfully to God's blessing on him. Most of us have felt God's blessing upon us at various times in our lives. Put yourself in Jacob's place. What would your response be? Do you think Jacob's reaction is a normal one? How have you responded to God's blessings on you?

Genesis 28:20-22—Bargaining With God

In these verses, Jacob makes a vow to God. Jacob says that if God will stay with him and provide for his basic needs, then he will remain faithful to God. Today we would call Jacob's vow a bargain. Is the bargain Jacob strikes with God at Bethel too calculated? Does Jacob make religious faith serve his own personal interests too much?

Have you ever said to God, "If you will just do this one thing for me, I will be faithful to you forever," or "If you will just get me through this crisis, I promise never to do it again?" What kinds of offers do you make in these bargains? What do you ask of God in return? Are these kinds of bargains all right to make with God? Do you think God responds favorably to our attempts at bargaining with him?

Genesis 31:36-42—Vocational Hardships

This passage gives one of the clearest pictures of the hardships of a shepherd's life. Jacob tells about the severe life of the shepherd. He is exposed to the elements, works long hours, and is threatened by wild beasts. Few of us have first-hand knowledge about what the life of a shepherd is like. But we can all identify with Jacob's experience of vocational hardships. How would you describe your work to Laban? What hardships are (or were) characteristic of your occupation?

Genesis 31:43-54—Honoring Our Agreements

In 31:43, Laban responds to all Jacob's complaints. Jacob has taken Laban's daughters, his flocks, and more. Laban sees Jacob's caravan of people, animals, and goods as his own, as rightfully belonging to Laban. But he is powerless and has to let Jacob go with all of these riches! Laban has finally met his match; his greed and trickery have not succeeded.

Jacob and Laban both have their faults. They have both resorted to trickery and deceit. Do you think that Jacob and Laban will honor their agreement with each other? Why or why not? Do your commitments to covenants that you make depend on the trustworthiness of the other persons involved?

For to see your face is like seeing the face of God (33:10).

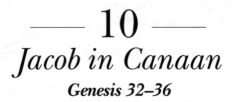

—— 10 ——
Jacob in Canaan
Genesis 32–36

DIMENSION ONE:
WHAT DOES THE BIBLE SAY?

Answer these questions by reading Genesis 32

1. Whom does Jacob encounter on his way home? (Genesis 32:1)

2. What does Jacob do when he hears that Esau and his men are coming? (Genesis 32:7)

3. What does Jacob include in his present to Esau? (Genesis 32:14-15)

4. What happens when Jacob wrestles with the man until daybreak? (Genesis 32:25)

5. What new name does God give Jacob at the Jabbok ford? (Genesis 32:28)

6. How does the wrestling match at the ford of the Jabbok River affect Jacob physically? (Genesis 32:31)

Answer these questions by reading Genesis 33

7. What is Esau's attitude toward Jacob when the two meet? (Genesis 33:4)

8. Why does Jacob not choose to accompany Esau on his journey? (Genesis 33:13-14)

9. Where does Jacob go after Esau and his men disappear? (Genesis 33:17-18)

Answer these questions by reading Genesis 34

10. Who falls in love with Jacob's daughter Dinah? (Genesis 34:2-3)

11. What do the sons of Jacob demand that the men of Shechem do in order to intermarry? (Genesis 34:15-17)

12. Which two sons of Jacob take the lead in attacking the men of Shechem? (Genesis 34:25-26)

13. Where does Jacob place the foreign gods of the people? (Genesis 35:4)

14. Where does Jacob bury Rachel? (Genesis 35:19-20)

15. How old is Isaac when he dies? (Genesis 35:28-29)

Answer these questions by reading Genesis 36

16. What are the names of Esau's five sons? (Genesis 36:4-5)

17. Where does Esau settle down with his family and possessions? (Genesis 36:8)

DIMENSION TWO:
WHAT DOES THE BIBLE MEAN?

❏ *Genesis 32:1-2.* Here the Hebrew word *Mahanaim** means "two armies" or "two companies" (of angels). Ancient peoples were greatly interested in the meanings of place names. The location named Mahanaim was part of the territory of the tribe of Gad in later times.

❏ *Genesis 32:22-32.* These verses contain the well-known story of Jacob's wrestling with God in the night. Jacob does not realize he is wrestling with God; he believes he is wrestling with a "man." Only after the experience is over does Jacob realize that he has wrestled with God. The story explains the name Peniel* or Penuel, a location on the Jabbok River.* The word *Peniel* or *Penuel* means "the face of God," which refers to Jacob's confronting God in his wrestling match.

In verse 26, Jacob asks for and receives a blessing from God. In addition to the blessing, something even more significant happens to Jacob at the Jabbok River. God changes his name from Jacob to Israel.* We read in verse 20 that Jacob's new name signifies his having striven with God and prevailed. As with Abraham and Sarah, Jacob's new name represents his new status before God.

❑ *Genesis 33:12-14.* The explanation Jacob gives for not going along with Esau is a credible one. When the new lambs and kids are still young, the flocks move slowly. But, of course, Jacob's real reason for not accompanying Esau has nothing to do with the condition of the flocks. Jacob is on his way back to the land of Canaan, where God's promise will be realized.

❑ *Genesis 33:17.* This verse explains the Hebrew name *Succoth.* * The word means "booths," and the city got its name from Israel's encampments in booths. The making of booths for cattle is not uncommon. The shepherd provides temporary shelter for the cattle during the rainy days by making roofed huts from tree branches.

❑ *Genesis 33:18-20.* Shechem is one of the important old Canaanite towns of Palestine. The city seems to have been one of the headquarters of the patriarchs in central Canaan. The reference to Jacob's arriving *safely* at Shechem may allude to his having been forced to fight a battle in the general region. Genesis 48:22 refers to a battle Jacob fought in the Shechem area. The words *mountain slope* are *Shechem* in Hebrew.

*The sons of Hamor** may mean "sons of the covenant," since the word *Hamor* means "donkey" in Hebrew. We know from Mesopotamian texts that "to kill a donkey" is the equivalent of "to make a covenant." This information suggests that the people of Shechem enter into a covenant with the Israelites. Therefore, this short reference to Jacob's buying land from the sons of Hamor has a great deal of religious importance.

❑ *Genesis 34:1-2.* We have read nothing about Dinah* before now, except that she was born to Leah and Jacob after they already had six sons. (See Genesis 30:21.) Genesis 34 is the only story about Dinah anywhere in the Old Testament.

The writer tells us that Hamor is a *Hivite.** The Septuagint (the Greek translation of the Old Testament made in Egypt) reads *Horite.** Horite is probably the Hebrew word for the Hurrian peoples, who were a people widely scattered throughout the ancient Near East.

❏ *Genesis 34:20-24.* We do not know if Shechem, like several other Canaanite cities, had an upper stratum of citizens who were non-Semites, but probably it did. The names of some Shechemites known from nonbiblical documents found at Shechem appear to be non-Semitic names. If so, these non-Semitic people may not have practiced circumcision.

Hamor proposes a general arrangement that will permit intermarriage between the Shechemites and the Israelites. The story indicates that the Israelites never seriously intended to accept this arrangement. They only agree to it in order to trick the Shechemites and get revenge on them for what the prince did to their sister Dinah.

❏ *Genesis 35:1-4.* Many scholars believe this story of Jacob's leaving Shechem for Bethel belongs to a tradition of ceremonial marching from Shechem to Bethel, as the Israelites moved their religious headquarters from Shechem to Bethel. Notice that the people perform seemingly religious acts. They purify themselves, change their clothing, and put the foreign gods under the oak tree at Shechem.

❏ *Genesis 35:5.* This verse mentions a *terror of God** that falls on the nearby cities during Jacob's journey from Shechem to Bethel. This terror of God may be connected with the religious acts of pilgrimage mentioned above. Holy seasons like the one described here were thought to be marked by special protection from the deity.

This terror of God refers to a kind of general panic on the part of Israel's enemies. When God puts them into this state, they are unable to organize themselves for defense against the Israelite army. In Exodus 23:27, God promises to inflict this terror on the enemies of his people so that Israel will prevail over them in battle.

❑ *Genesis 35:8.* The story of Deborah's* death and burial under the oak tree explains why persons weep regularly at this oak tree. The name *Allon Bacuth* that is given to this tree means "oak of weeping."* Ritual weeping connected with agricultural rites probably occurred at this place of worship. Ritual weeping over the earth's barrenness often accompanied the ceremonies that ushered in the rainy season of the early fall.

❑ *Genesis 35:16-20.* Rachel gives birth to Benjamin* in the land of Canaan. He is the last of Jacob's children. Rachel dies in giving birth to Benjamin, which helps to explain why this son is so important to Jacob. Today, the tomb of Rachel still stands on the main highway from Jerusalem, north of Bethlehem.

❑ *Genesis 35:21.* This verse tells us that Jacob journeys on, after Rachel's death and burial, and stops somewhere "beyond Migdal Eder."* In Hebrew this name means something like "cattle tower" and refers to a primitive structure built by shepherds. The tower of Eder is probably somewhere near Jerusalem.

❑ *Genesis 35:22.* The brief story of Reuben's sinning with Jacob's concubine, Bilhah, will echo in Jacob's blessing of Reuben. In Genesis 49:3-4, Jacob denies Reuben the pre-eminence that would normally have been his as the first-born son. Jacob also denies Simeon and Levi pre-eminence because of their misdeeds against the inhabitants of the city of Shechem. (See Genesis 34:25-29; 49:4-7.)

❑ *Genesis 35:27-29.* Jacob now moves on to Hebron, his location when the Joseph story begins in Genesis 37. Esau and Jacob join forces one more time when they bury their father Isaac. But from this time forward, Esau and Jacob do not meet again.

❑ *Genesis 36.* This chapter gives a full genealogy of Esau. This genealogy shows that the old traditions do not entirely ignore the son who lost his birthright and blessing. First is a genealogy of the descendants of Esau born in Canaan (Genesis 36:1-5). Then we read that Esau breaks definitively with Jacob and the land promised to Jacob and his descendants. He moves to the land of Edom, a territory south of the Dead Sea.

DIMENSION THREE:
WHAT DOES THE BIBLE MEAN TO ME?

Genesis 32–36 contains at least three issues that have meaning for our lives today.

Genesis 32:1-21—Appeasement or Bribery?

Genesis 32 describes rather fully Jacob's efforts to prevent Esau from doing him harm. Jacob sends his messengers first to warn Esau that he is coming and to ask Esau to welcome him warmly. Jacob prays to God to deliver him from Esau's wrath. He gathers over five hundred animals for Esau as a present. He then instructs his servants about how to make the journey and give Esau the present.

Verse 20 tells us the reason for Jacob's extensive preparations for the reunion. He wants to appease Esau—to soothe his anger. Do you think the storyteller wants us to understand that Jacob knows he mistreated his brother over the birthright and the blessing? Is Jacob sorry for what he did? Or is he simply being his usual self, anticipating Esau's anger and finding a way to turn the anger aside?

Try to put yourself in Esau's place. Remembering Jacob's past actions, how would you interpret his attempts at appeasement? Would you think Jacob was trying to bribe you? Or would you see his actions as a genuine attempt at reconciliation? When in your life have you been in the position of Esau? of Jacob?

Genesis 32:22-32—Encounters With God

The story of Jacob's encounter with God by the Jabbok River has puzzled generations of Bible readers. Persons have identified the religious significance of this event in many different ways. Is Jacob a changed person after this encounter? Does he learn to place his trust in God in a different way than before?

Have you had an encounter with God that has changed your life? If so, was the change in you a visible one? How would you describe the change to someone else? Do all encounters with God result in changes that others can see?

Genesis 34:1-31—The Cycle of Crime

This chapter opens with a brief account of Shechem's crime against Dinah. Jacob's sons—Dinah's brothers—become very angry with Shechem when they discover what he has done. Verse 13 tells us that Jacob's sons deal with Hamor and Shechem deceitfully. They pretend they will go along with the plan to intermarry with the Shechemites, but they have no intention of doing so.

Why do Dinah's brothers deceive the Shechemites—because they are angry about the humiliation of their sister? How do they get revenge on Shechem and his father Hamor? Verses 25 and 26 tell us that Simeon and Levi come quietly into the city and kill all the males, including Shechem and Hamor. Is the crime of Simeon and Levi justified by Shechem's crime against Dinah?

Can you think of instances where one crime has resulted in another, with no clear way to break the cycle? What is your reaction to these situations?

Now Israel loved Joseph more than any of his other sons (37:3).

— 11 —
Joseph's Journey to Egypt
Genesis 37–41

DIMENSION ONE:
WHAT DOES THE BIBLE SAY?

Answer these questions by reading Genesis 37

1. What garment does Joseph's father give him? (Genesis 37:3)

2. Why do Joseph's brothers hate him? (Genesis 37:4)

3. How do Joseph's brothers interpret Joseph's first dream? (Genesis 37:6-8)

4. What does Joseph's father understand the second dream to mean? (Genesis 37:9-10)

5. Which brother intervenes to save Joseph's life? (Genesis 37:21)

6. Who proposes that the brothers sell Joseph to the Ishmaelites? (Genesis 37:26-27)

7. What do the brothers do to Joseph's robe? (Genesis 37:31-33)

8. Who buys Joseph in Egypt? (Genesis 37:36)

Answer these questions by reading Genesis 38

9. Whom does Judah choose for his eldest son Er to marry? (Genesis 38:6)

10. After Er and Onan die, what does Judah ask Tamar to do? (Genesis 38:11)

11. What does Tamar do in order to bear a child in memory of her husband, Er? (Genesis 38:14-19)

12. How does Tamar convince Judah that he is the father of her son? (Genesis 38:18, 25-26)

Answer these questions by reading Genesis 39

13. How does Joseph fare in Potiphar's house? (Genesis 39:2-6)

14. How does Joseph respond to his master's wife when she tempts him? (Genesis 39:8-10)

Answer these questions by reading Genesis 40

15. Whom does Pharaoh imprison with Joseph? (Genesis 40:1-3)

16. What are Joseph's duties while in prison? (Genesis 40:4)

17. Who interprets the dreams of those imprisoned by the pharaoh? (Genesis 40:8-19)

18. What does the pharaoh do to the chief cupbearer and the chief baker? (Genesis 40:21-22)

19. To whom does Pharaoh first send to interpret his dreams? (Genesis 41:8)

20. How does Joseph interpret Pharaoh's dreams? (Genesis 41:25-36)

21. Whom does Pharaoh place in charge of preparations for the time of famine? (Genesis 41:37-45)

22. What does Joseph do during the seven years of plenty? (Genesis 41:47-49)

23. What does Joseph do when the people face famine? (Genesis 41:55-57)

DIMENSION TWO: WHAT DOES THE BIBLE MEAN?

❏ *Genesis 37:2-4.* Due to our inability to translate the Hebrew accurately, we can only speculate about Joseph's robe. Probably the "richly ornamented robe" is a type of dress worn by those who do no heavy work. Joseph is not a shepherd like his brothers, nor does he tend the grainfields. He is his father's favorite, and he stays at home and plays. The garment he sports, therefore, singles him out as his father's darling.

JOSEPH'S JOURNEY TO EGYPT   **81**

❑ *Genesis 37:15-17.* Joseph's wandering in the fields near Shechem tells us that he does not really know how to manage in the countryside away from home. The journey on to Dothan,* about thirteen miles to the north of Shechem, is apparently Joseph's idea.

❑ *Genesis 37:28.* Verse 28 poses some problems. Three groups are involved in the sale of Joseph: the brothers, the Midianites,* and the Ishmaelites.* However, in verse 36 of the same chapter, we read that the Midianites sell Joseph to Potiphar* in Egypt. This confusion about who is selling to whom results from the mingling of two traditions—one that involved the Midianites and another that involved the Ishmaelites. For our writer's purposes, the two groups are synonymous. So Joseph's brothers sell Joseph to the Ishmaelites, or Midianite traders.

❑ *Genesis 37:29-31.* This passage gives us a clear picture of the underhandedness of Joseph's brothers. Reuben, the brother who initially pleads for Joseph's life, actually intends to come back later to rescue Joseph and restore him to his father (verse 22). Apparently, while Reuben is away, his brothers devise this scheme of selling Joseph to the traders. Reuben returns to the pit, discovers it is empty, and turns in despair to his brothers. They do not in any way set his mind at ease, even though they know what has happened to Joseph. They simply suggest an alternate way of handling the situation.

❑ *Genesis 38:1.* Suddenly we confront a story that does not seem to fit into the events of Joseph's life. This story about Judah* and Tamar* seems to come from a separate tradition. Apparently the writer places it here in order to keep the stories in rough chronological order.

Judah suffers from his refusal to follow marriage customs with his daughter-in-law. The story also offers a kind of interlude in the Joseph story, giving Joseph time to settle in Egypt in the home of his master. This time lapse prepares us for Joseph's transformation from a young spoiled brat into a wise and faithful servant of God.

❑ *Genesis 38:6-11.* Er's premature death leaves no descendants in the family. Onan,* the brother of Er,* refuses to give Tamar a child, and God slays him. Tamar patiently waits for years for Judah to give her his third son as a husband. This process is in accordance with the law found in Deuteronomy 25:5-10. Onan's crime is his refusal to provide a descendant to bear his dead brother's name.

❑ *Genesis 38:12-19.* Tamar then resorts to prostitution—the only way by which she can have a child and thereby remove her own sense of failure at not having borne her husband an heir. When Tamar hears that her father-in-law is coming, she disguises herself as a harlot. The pledge that Tamar requests from Judah, his signet, cord, and staff, will later be proof of Judah's dealings with a "prostitute."

❑ *Genesis 38:27-30.* The story of the birth of Tamar's twins, with the detail about which is born first, indicates how important it was in ancient times to know which child was the first-born. One of the midwife's duties is to make certain which twin comes first. The father's inheritance is larger for the first-born, and the eldest becomes the head of the household under certain circumstances.

❑ *Genesis 40:1-3.* The terms *chief cupbearer** and *chief baker** refer to high officials in the court of the pharaoh.* These English translations are a bit misleading. The cupbearer has charge of the wine for the royal table. He is a trusted high official who is also responsible for ceremonial leadership in the household. The chief baker is probably responsible for protocol, ceremonies, banquets, and the like.

❑ *Genesis 41:25-32.* We might suppose that storing up grain for lean years is a practical matter of business. Why does Pharaoh need a special dream to warn him of coming famine? In Egypt the Nile overflows its banks at the same time each year. Even if the rainy season brings less rain than normal, the rains do not fail entirely. Thus, only an extraordinary occurrence would bring about a seven-year famine in Egypt.

We also need to realize that normally Egypt would not experience seven good years. A sameness of the harvest in Egypt makes this story of seven fat years followed by seven lean years difficult to fit into the economic and agricultural pattern of Egypt. The story is more easily understood from the vantage point of Canaan, the homeland of its writer. In Canaan, the idea of seven fat years followed by seven lean years fits the agricultural conditions very well.

JOSEPH'S JOURNEY TO EGYPT   **83**

❏ *Genesis 41:40-45.* Here the pharaoh authorizes Joseph to be his representative. In addition, the pharaoh places Joseph in charge of the day-to-day affairs of the palace. The ring and chain that Pharaoh gives Joseph symbolize Joseph's position of honor.

DIMENSION THREE:
WHAT DOES THE BIBLE MEAN TO ME?

The first part of the Joseph story, Genesis 37–41, raises three issues that have meaning for our lives today.

Genesis 37:1-11—Sibling Rivalry

Joseph's family difficulties stem from his own character, from his boasting dreams, and from his father's doting love of him. Joseph is a homebody and does not regularly shepherd the flocks or farm the fields. With his half-brothers, the children of the servants Bilhah and Zilpah, he plays in the settlement of his father. His bad reports about the activities of his half-brothers anger them. He dreams of his ascendancy over his brothers and his father and mother, and angers everyone. Yet his father gives him an elaborate coat, thus tingeing the anger of his brothers with envy and hatred.

Many family situations are characterized by such sibling rivalry. You may remember having feelings of rivalry toward your brothers and sisters, or you may have children in your family who do not always get along. What can parents do to remedy these situations? What can children do? Do you think sibling rivalry is inevitable when there is more than one child in the family?

Genesis 38—Women's Rights

When Er, Tamar's first husband, dies, Judah orders Onan, the dead man's brother, to perform his brotherly duty. Since offspring were highly desired, the duty of a widow's brother-in-law was to help her produce children—male children in particular. The males then carry on the family name. The widow apparently has no choice in this arrangement.

You can read about this law, called the law of *levirate marriage,** in Deuteronomy 25:5-10. Imagine yourself as a young widow in Tamar's situation, or as the brother-in-law of Tamar. How would you react to Judah's instruction? Do you think this levirate law protects women or takes away their rights?

Genesis 39:1-6—The Providence of God

These verses show Joseph's prosperity in Egypt and his success as overseer of the pharaoh's house. The Bible tells us that Joseph's situation results from the fact that God is with him. Do you think that Joseph's prosperity, his always coming out on top, is fair? Do you know persons who always seem to land on their feet no matter what happens, who seem to be the favorites of God? How do you account for such instances?

At times in your life you may have thought of yourself as one of God's favorites. At other times, perhaps you have felt the absence of God in your life. Is the providence of God only visible to you during the good times? When have you doubted the providence of God in your life?

It was to save lives that God sent me ahead of you (45:5).

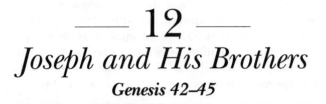

—— **12** ——
Joseph and His Brothers
Genesis 42–45

DIMENSION ONE:
WHAT DOES THE BIBLE SAY?

Answer these questions by reading Genesis 42

1. Why does Jacob not allow Benjamin to go to Egypt?
   (Genesis 42:4)

2. What does Joseph give as the reason for his brothers'
   coming into the land of Egypt? (Genesis 42:9, 12, 14)

3. Whom does Joseph keep as a hostage when he lets the
   brothers return to Canaan with grain? (Genesis 42:19, 24)

4. How are the brothers to obtain the release of Simeon?
   (Genesis 42:20)

5. How does Reuben's rebuke of the other brothers for their
   mistreatment of Joseph, affect Joseph? (Genesis 42:24)

6. What do the brothers discover in the tops of their bags of grain? (Genesis 42:27)

7. How does Jacob respond to the demand that the brothers take Benjamin to Egypt? (Genesis 42:38)

Answer these questions by reading Genesis 43

8. Why does Jacob send his sons to Egypt a second time? (Genesis 43:1-2)

9. How does Judah get his father to agree to let the brothers take Benjamin with them? (Genesis 43:4-10)

10. How does Jacob try to prevent the Egyptians from keeping Simeon and Benjamin? (Genesis 43:11-14)

11. Why do the brothers think they are brought to Joseph's house? (Genesis 43:18)

12. What does Joseph do when he sees Benjamin? (Genesis 43:29-30)

13. What kind of portion do the servants give Benjamin? (Genesis 43:34)

Answer these questions by reading Genesis 44

14. What does Joseph order his steward to place in Benjamin's bag, along with the grain and the money? (Genesis 44:2)

15. How do the brothers react when Joseph's steward finds the cup in Benjamin's sack? (Genesis 44:13)

16. Who does Joseph say will be his slave? (Genesis 44:17)

17. What does Judah offer to do to free Benjamin? (Genesis 44:33)

Answer these questions by reading Genesis 45

18. How does Joseph explain his brothers' deed? (Genesis 45:5, 7, 8)

19. What does Joseph tell his brothers to do? (Genesis 45:9)

20. What is the pharaoh's reaction to the news that Joseph's brothers have come to Egypt? (Genesis 45:16-20)

DIMENSION TWO:
WHAT DOES THE BIBLE MEAN?

❏ *Genesis 42:1.* The constant flow of the Nile gives Egypt possibilities of life that drought and famine could eliminate in other parts of the ancient Near East. Even without the special measures taken by Joseph, Egypt would have food. But our story builds the drama by underscoring the extent of the famine. "The famine was severe in all the world" (Genesis 41:57).

Jacob's words, "Why do you just keep looking at one another?" probably mean something like "Why do you stand here looking blankly at one another? Why don't you *do* something?" We would say, "Don't just stand there, do something!"

❏ *Genesis 42:3-4.* Sending ten of the brothers and leaving only Benjamin at home is also necessary for the dramatic effect. Joseph will play cat and mouse with his brothers, punishing them for their treatment of him and also teaching them a severe lesson. All the brothers except Benjamin go to Egypt, and the drama begins to unfold.

❏ *Genesis 42:9-13.* Joseph's claim that his brothers have come to spy out the land is part of Joseph's plan to keep them off balance. He wants to keep them guessing about his intentions, and he wants to confront them with a situation they cannot control. The brothers know they are not foreign spies; who could suppose that they are? But if Joseph insists that they are spies, what can they possibly say to convince him otherwise? The brothers realize they are powerless.

JOSEPH AND HIS BROTHERS

So Joseph's brothers defend themselves by telling their family story. They talk about their father, their youngest brother, and the other brother who is no more. How ironic that the other brother who is no more is standing right in front of them! In addition to teaching his brothers a lesson, Joseph also learns about the welfare of his family without asking.

❏ *Genesis 42:18-24.* The brothers confer freely before Joseph, never dreaming that he knows their language and understands what they are saying. Their confession of guilt in dealing with Joseph, and Reuben's "Didn't I tell you?" are too much for Joseph temporarily; he has to turn aside and weep. But then he recovers himself and proceeds with the charade.

❏ *Genesis 42:36-38.* When Jacob learns that Simeon is being held hostage for Benjamin, his reaction is a mixture of anger and grief. He cannot treat Simeon's loss casually, and yet he cannot bring himself to let Benjamin go. Jacob rejects Reuben's offer of his two sons as surety for the life of Benjamin. We cannot help but feel that Jacob's favoritism for Benjamin wounds the other sons deeply.

The expression "bring my gray head down to the grave" simply means that the loss of Benjamin would be more than an old man should be asked to bear.

❏ *Genesis 43:1-10.* The famine continues, and Jacob is forced to ask his sons to go to Egypt once more and buy grain. The brothers point out that they cannot get any more grain unless they meet the Egyptian's demands. Jacob has to relent, and Judah offers assurance while displaying considerable impatience with his father. We have wasted enough time talking about the matter to have gone to Egypt and back, twice over!

❏ *Genesis 43:11-12.* Jacob sends rich presents to the Egyptian to soften his heart so that he will do Benjamin no harm and also release Simeon. It seems like a very rich gift for a family about to perish from famine. These items were probably the hoardings of the family in a time of deprivation. These possessions are a great treasure to Jacob and his family, but of little consequence materially to the Egyptian.

❏ *Genesis 43:16-18.* The storyteller passes over the trip to Egypt in silence. The brothers are immediately in Egypt, appearing at Joseph's house. Joseph arranges for the brothers to be his guests for dinner at the noon hour. Of course the preparations Joseph makes for them appear ominous to the brothers. What will this strange Egyptian do to us, or demand from us now?

❑ *Genesis 42:24-25.* The tension mounts as the brothers wait for the meeting with Joseph. What will the meal with him be like? Is he really preparing a feast for them? Or will he humiliate them and take Benjamin? The brothers are completely at the mercy of these officials of the pharaoh.

Washing the feet is a customary part of the preparation for the meal taken indoors. One removes the sandals as one enters the house, and the feet are washed by a servant. The brothers now await Joseph's coming.

❑ *Genesis 43:26-34.* This passage describes the banquet scene in detail. Joseph sits alone at one table, the Egyptians are at another table, and the brothers of Joseph occupy a third table. The Egyptians have dietary customs that do not allow them to eat with foreigners. The serving of food from Joseph's table to the guests accords with ancient custom. We can well imagine that Joseph keeps the servants busy bringing food and drink to the brothers.

❑ *Genesis 44:1-2.* Joseph arranges for his silver cup to be hidden in Benjamin's sack of grain. The importance of his cup does not lie in its monetary value. This cup is a divining cup,* and therefore a sacred object. Supposedly small objects placed in the liquid of the cup enable a diviner to tell the future. Other commentators suggest various uses for his divining cup, but we do know that it was important to Joseph. Once again, Joseph is playing with his brothers, punishing them for their mistreatment of him.

❑ *Genesis 44:16.* Judah's confession of guilt apparently comes about as he realizes that resistance to anything Joseph says will be futile. He confesses a guilt that he does not feel and does not have, but what else can he do? They did not steal the silver cup, but there it is! Joseph states that all of the brothers except Benjamin are free to return to their father. Benjamin must remain.

❑ *Genesis 44:18-34.* Judah's powerful plea for his brother is one of the most beautiful parts of the story. Perhaps it is the author's way of showing that Joseph has done enough to avenge himself on the brothers. Keeping Benjamin would mean death for the aged father. Let Judah remain, but let Benjamin go free.

❑ *Genesis 45:10-20.* The land of Goshen* is to the east of the Nile delta, on the edge of the farmed acreage. Joseph arranges for Jacob and his sons to settle there and live out the years of famine under Joseph's care and protection. The pharaoh confirms Joseph's decision. Pharaoh goes even farther than Joseph in welcoming Jacob and his family to Egypt, giving them special presents.

DIMENSION THREE:
WHAT DOES THE BIBLE MEAN TO ME?

The conclusion of the Joseph story, Genesis 42–45, provides at least two questions that are relevant for our lives today.

Genesis 42:6-28—Revenge

Joseph clearly intends that his brothers be punished for what they did to him. Verse 7 tells us that he treats them like strangers and speaks roughly to them. Joseph devises a careful plan that he uses to get revenge on his brothers.

First, Joseph falsely accuses the brothers of coming to Egypt in order to spy out the land for a later attack. Then he tells them that they may not return to their home unless they bring their youngest brother, Benjamin, to Egypt. Joseph eavesdrops on his brothers' conversation, since they do not know that Joseph can understand what they are saying. Also, Joseph takes Simeon from them and keeps him in prison. And finally, Joseph secretly puts their money back into their sacks, so that they will fear Joseph's accusation that they stole the money.

These verses show Joseph as a person with a long memory, who willingly takes revenge on his unsuspecting brothers. Do you think that Joseph toys with his brothers too much and too long? Think about the times in your life when you felt mistreated by others. Did you feel vengeful as Joseph did? How did you act on these feelings of vengeance?

Genesis 45:1-15—The Guidance of God

In this moving scene of Joseph's reunion with his brothers, he makes the point that God has been directing the events in their lives. Joseph tells his brothers not to be afraid, because God is responsible for their situation. God sent Joseph to Egypt; the brothers have no reason to fear.

Can you relate to Joseph's understanding of God working through his brothers' misdeed in order to send him to Egypt? Does Joseph believe a divine purpose is at work within his brothers' wrong act? Or does Joseph believe that the entire event was God's doing from first to last?

Have you experienced God's guidance in the negative situations of your life? If so, was God's presence real to you at the time? Or were you aware of God's guidance only when you looked back on the experience at a later time?

I am God, the God of your father. . . . Do not be afraid to go down to Egypt, for I will make you into a great nation there (46:3).

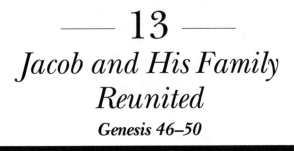

—— 13 ——
Jacob and His Family Reunited
Genesis 46–50

DIMENSION ONE:
WHAT DOES THE BIBLE SAY?

Answer these questions by reading Genesis 46

1. Including those who are born in Egypt, how many persons make up Jacob's household? (Genesis 46:26-27)

2. Why does Joseph tell his father and brothers to tell Pharaoh that they are shepherds? (Genesis 46:34)

Answer these questions by reading Genesis 47

3. When the Egyptians have no more money to buy grain, what does Joseph first take from them in place of money? (Genesis 47:16-17)

4. When their cattle and other animals are gone, what do the Egyptians next give to Joseph in exchange for grain? (Genesis 47:18-19)

5. What land does Joseph not buy up for the pharaoh? (Genesis 47:22)

6. What portion of the grain do the people give to Pharaoh? (Genesis 47:24-26)

7. What does Jacob make Joseph swear to do after Jacob's death? (Genesis 47:29-30)

Answer these questions by reading Genesis 48

8. What does Joseph do when he hears that his father is ill? (Genesis 48:1-2)

9. Which of Joseph's two sons receives the greater blessing from Jacob? (Genesis 48:13-20)

Answer these questions by reading Genesis 49

10. Who is Jacob's first-born son? (Genesis 49:3)

11. Why does Jacob curse Simeon and Levi? (Genesis 49:7)

12. How will Judah's brothers treat him in the future? (Genesis 49:8)

13. Which of Jacob's sons receives the greatest blessing? (Genesis 49:22-26)

14. Where does Jacob demand that his sons bury him? (Genesis 49:29-31)

Answer these questions by reading Genesis 50

15. What does Joseph have done to his father's body in Egypt? (Genesis 50:2-3)

16. Where do Joseph and the mourning party stop to weep for Jacob? (Genesis 50:10-11)

17. What do Joseph's brothers fear from Joseph after the death of their father? (Genesis 50:15)

18. How does Joseph explain his brothers' mistreatment of him? (Genesis 50:20)

DIMENSION TWO: WHAT DOES THE BIBLE MEAN?

❏ *Genesis 46:1-4.* Here Jacob begins his journey from Hebron to Egypt. He apparently stops at Beersheba to secure the approval of God for his journey into Egypt. This journey of Jacob and his family is the beginning of a new era in the lives of God's chosen people, and the writer emphasizes God's active role in Jacob's departure from Hebron.

❏ *Genesis 46:8-27.* The writer carefully constructs Jacob's genealogy to show the descendants who counted in the regular lineage from Jacob. These descendants number sixty-six persons, plus Jacob himself, Joseph, and Joseph's two sons, for a total of seventy. A summary of this list appears at the beginning of the Book of Exodus, but the number seventy is included since it is an important part of the tradition. (See Exodus 1:1-5.)

❏ *Genesis 46:29.* Imagine this reunion between Joseph and his father Jacob, who has thought his son to be dead for the last twenty-two years! Falling on a person's neck means to embrace and is a part of the social custom of the Near East to this day.

❏ *Genesis 46:31-34.* Verse 34 tells us that shepherds are not welcome in Egypt, since shepherds are detestable to the Egyptians. This attitude is understandable from the viewpoint of the farmers who till the arable land in the delta region and along the banks of the Nile. However, shepherds were very important in ancient Egypt. The wool of the sheep and the food provided by the flocks were critical to the Egyptian economy.

We probably have two traditions here. One tradition spoke of the Israelites as herders of cattle, so that they would be more welcome in the land of Goshen. The other tradition spoke of the Israelites as shepherds, but pointed to their ability to tend cattle as well. Notice that in Genesis 47:6, the pharaoh gives instructions that any capable persons among the Israelites should be given responsibility for his own herds.

❑ *Genesis 47:20-26.* The priests receive special treatment—Joseph does not buy their land since they have a fixed income that they receive from Pharaoh. We know that in ancient Egyptian society, the priests had great influence and so were singled out for special treatment. Notice that the "tenant farmers" do retain four-fifths of their harvest. Perhaps the story intends to show us Joseph's humane treatment of those under his control.

❑ *Genesis 47:27-31.* Jacob continues to live in Egypt, enjoying the favor of Joseph and the pharaoh long after the famine ends. Whereas at the end of Chapter 45 we read that Jacob expects to die in the near future (Genesis 45:28), in 47:28 we learn that Jacob lives in Egypt for seventeen years.

❑ *Genesis 48:1-7.* The Bible seems to preserve the story about the blessing of Manasseh* and Ephraim* in two parts. The first part (verses 1-7) presents Jacob as claiming Manasseh and Ephraim as his own sons, making them part of his twelve sons and thus part of the twelve tribes of Israel. This tradition reflects the practice of naming not Joseph but Ephraim and Manasseh among the descendants.

❑ *Genesis 48:8-19.* The other story of the blessing deals with which of the two sons will have pre-eminence. Joseph wants Jacob to bless Manasseh as the first-born. But Jacob insists on letting the primary blessing—symbolized by the right hand—go to Ephraim. This story probably reflects the actual ascendancy of the tribe of Ephraim over that of Manasseh in later centuries.

❑ *Genesis 49:1-2.* Jacob's blessing of his sons prior to his death represents an important kind of literature for ancient Israel. At the time of approaching death, the dying head of the family was understood to have special powers. These powers might include the ability to foretell the future fates of individuals or groups. Or they might include visions that normally are hidden from the eyes of the living. As we saw in the case of Isaac (Genesis 27), the power of these spoken blessings is immediate when the words are spoken in the right way and with the full strength of the dying patriarch.

Here in Genesis 49, the blessing of Jacob covers the characters of his twelve sons, including Levi. Since Jacob includes Levi among the twelve, he does not substitute Manasseh and Ephraim for Joseph (see the discussion above under Genesis 48:1-7). Most of Jacob's blessings carry a sting with them, a criticism of the sons for not quite fulfilling the destiny God had in store for them. Jacob singles out Judah and Joseph for special praise.

❏ *Genesis 49:8-12.* Jacob's blessing of Judah contains some royal terminology. For example, the *scepter* mentioned in verse 10 is a symbol of kingly power. Many commentators have pointed to parallels between this description of Judah and the Bible's portrayal of King David. Perhaps this blessing comes from the period when David was serving as king of Judah in Hebron—before he was crowned king of all Israel. (See 2 Samuel 1–4.)

❏ *Genesis 50:1-3.* We learn that Joseph's physicians embalm Jacob (here called Israel) after his death. Embalming was a costly and time-consuming process, reserved for those who could afford the cost.

❏ *Genesis 50:4-11.* The story of Jacob's burial has two parts. In the first part (verses 4-11), a great host of folk accompany Joseph and his brothers as they go to the threshing floor* of Atad.* This threshing floor is located "beyond the Jordan," which normally means the region east of the Jordan River.*

There the company mourns and laments Jacob for seven days. The place is thereafter named Abel Mizraim, understood to mean the "mourning of the Egyptians." These verses indicate that the sons bury Jacob at this location, rather than with his grandfather and father in the cave of Machpelah, near Hebron.

❏ *Genesis 50:12-14.* These verses contain the second part of the story of Jacob's burial. Here Jacob's sons bury him in the cave at Machpelah—the standard tradition. We probably have two rival traditions as to where Jacob was buried. These traditions are now harmonized by making the threshing floor of Atad into a spot where the Egyptians and the family of Jacob stop in order to mourn Jacob for seven days.

❑ *Genesis 50:22-26.* To have children born upon one's knee means to be present at the birth, to receive the child, and to name it. Joseph lives long enough to see his grandchildren and great-grandchildren.

Joseph makes arrangements for his sons to embalm his body and take his bones with them back to the land of Canaan. Only hundreds of years later do Joseph's bones reach his homeland. In the closing verses of the Book of Joshua we read that the people of Israel bury Joseph's bones at Shechem, in the land his father purchased from the sons of Hamor. (See Joshua 24:32.)

DIMENSION THREE: WHAT DOES THE BIBLE MEAN TO ME?

Genesis 46–50 gives us three questions that call for a response in our lives today.

Genesis 46:1-4—Trusting in God's Promises

In these verses, God tells Jacob not to be afraid to go down to Egypt. Why do you think God gives this assurance? Was Jacob's leaving the land of Canaan a denial of God's promise? Remember that in Genesis 12 Abraham also left the land of Canaan when a famine struck. Is Jacob endangering God's promise by journeying to Egypt?

Think about what you would do in Jacob's place. You have just discovered that your favorite son, whom you have thought to be dead for many years, is still alive. Your first impulse is to go and see him. But what about God's promise that you would dwell in the land of Canaan? If you go to Egypt to see your son, are you going against God's wishes? What would you do?

Genesis 49:8-12—The Importance of Possessions

Genesis 49:8-12 contains the blessing of Judah, a passage that the church has treated as a messianic promise. These verses speak about "Shiloh" or "his ruler" or the one "to whom it belongs" (all these are possible translations of the difficult text in verse 10). He "to whom it belongs" will take leadership in Judah, and his reign will be marked by great blessing and plenty. Wine will be so plentiful that persons can wash their clothes in it. The ruler will have plenty of milk to drink and ample wine to make the eyes sparkle.

How does this picture of a messianic age sound today? Is it earthy, too much tied to material blessings? Or is it good for us to have such materialistic pictures of the fulfillment of God's work on earth? How much importance do you attach to your material possessions?

Genesis 50:15-21—Turning Evil Into Good

Many people find the main point of the Joseph stories in Genesis 50:20. Human beings propose, but God disposes. The brothers set out to get rid of Joseph because he angered and offended them. But God used their evil deed to save the lives of multitudes who otherwise would have starved when the famine came. God meant that deed for good, not approving it, but using it to bring about good. What events in your life have seemed evil, but have been used by God for good? Can we say that God *always* brings good out of evil?

GLOSSARY OF TERMS

Abel: the son of Adam and Eve, killed by his brother Cain, a shepherd by vocation (Genesis 4)

Abimelech: the king of Gerar, made a covenant with Abraham at Beersheba (Genesis 20; 21; 26)

Abraham: the son of Terah, father of Isaac, the first patriarch (Genesis 12–25)

Abram: the original name of Abraham, before God changed it to Abraham in 17:5 (Genesis 12–25)

Adam: the first man on the earth, placed by God in Eden (Genesis 3–5)

Ai: a city near Bethel; Abraham built an altar between Bethel and Ai (Genesis 12:8; 13:3)

Ammon: a territory east of the Jordan River

Ammonites: descendants of Lot who settled in Ammon (Genesis 19:38)

Amorites: various Semitic people who settled in Mesopotamia, Syria, and Palestine (Genesis 10:16; 14:7, 13; 15:16, 21; 48:22)

Ancient Near East: the southwestern part of Asia, including Egypt and Israel

Ararat: The mountain range on which Noah's ark came to rest (Genesis 8:4)

Arphaxad: the son of Shem, father of Shelah (Genesis 10:22, 24; 11:10-13)

Asher: the son of Jacob and Zilpah, ancestor of the tribe of Asher (Genesis 30:13; 35:26; 46:17; 49:20)

Atad: a place east of the Jordan River where Jacob's family stopped to mourn him for seven days (Genesis 50:10-11)

Babel: a city in the region of Shinar, synonymous with Babylon (Genesis 11:9)

Babylon: The capital of the Babylonian Empire, also called Shinar (see Genesis 10:10; 11:1-9)

Beersheba: a city in the southern part of Canaan, the site of Abraham's covenant with Abimelech (Genesis 21)

Benjamin: The son of Jacob and Rachel, ancestor of the tribe of Benjamin (Genesis 37–50)

Bethel: a city north of Jerusalem, called Luz by the Canaanites (Genesis 12:8; 13:3; 28:19; 31:13; 35)

Bethuel: the son of Nahor, father of Laban and Rebekah, nephew of Abraham (Genesis 24)

Bilhah: the handmaid of Rachel, mother of Dan and Naphtali (Genesis 29:29; 30:3-5, 7; 35:22; 37:2; 46:25)

Birthright: privileges belonging to the first-born son, sold to Jacob by Esau (Genesis 25)

Blessing: a wish or prayer that can actually come about by pronouncing it (Genesis 12:1-3; 27; 49)

Cain: the son of Adam and Eve, killed his brother Abel, a farmer by vocation (Genesis 4)

Canaan I: son of Ham, grandson of Noah (Genesis 9)

Canaan II: the land settled by Abraham and his descendants

Cherubim: winged creatures that guarded the tree of life at the east of Eden (Genesis 3:24)

Chief Baker: responsible for protocol in the court of the pharaoh (Genesis 40)

Chief Cupbearer: the butler in the pharaoh's court, who had charge of the wine for the royal table (Genesis 40)

Circumcision: a sign of membership in the covenant community (Genesis 17; 34)

GLOSSARY OF TERMS

City Gate: the main meeting place in ancient cities where cases of law were settled (Genesis 19:1; 23:10, 18; 34:20, 24)

Cities of the Plain: Sodom, Gomorrah, Admah, Zeboiim, and Zoar; all but Zoar were destroyed by God for their wickedness (Genesis 13:12; 19:29)

Covenant: an agreement between two parties (Genesis 6:18; 9:9-17; 15:18; 17; 21:27, 32; 26:28; 31:44)

Cubit: a measurement of the length of the forearm, about eighteen inches (Genesis 6:15, 16; 7:20)

Dan: the son of Jacob and Bilhah, ancestor of the tribe of Dan (Genesis 30:6; 35:25; 46:23; 49:16, 17)

Dead Sea: called the Salt Sea in Genesis, a body of water in southern Canaan (Genesis 14:3)

Deborah: the nurse of Rebekah, buried under the Oak of Weeping (Genesis 35:8)

Deep, The: the watery chaos that existed before God began the creation process (Genesis 1:1; 7:11; 8:2)

Dinah: the daughter of Jacob and Leah, who was raped by Shechem (Genesis 30:21; 34; 46:15)

Divine Assembly: beings that surround God in heaven and do God's bidding (Genesis 1:26)

Divining Cup: a sacred goblet that enabled its owner to foretell the future; Joseph accused his brothers of stealing his divining cup (Genesis 44)

Dothan: a town north of Shechem to which Joseph journeyed to find his brothers (Genesis 37:17)

Eastern People: a general expression referring to the Arabian neighbors to the east of Canaan (Genesis 29:1)

Eden: the garden in which God placed the first man (Genesis 2; 3:23-24; 4:16)

GLOSSARY OF TERMS

Edom I: Another name for Esau (Genesis 25:30)

Edom II: a region south of the Dead Sea, inhabited by the descendants of Esau (Genesis 36)

Egypt: a country southwest of Canaan

Elohim: in Hebrew, the general term for God

Enoch: the son of Cain, grandson of Adam (Genesis 4–5)

Enosh: the son of Seth, grandson of Adam (Genesis 4–5)

Ephraim: one of Joseph's two sons, born in Egypt, ancestor of the tribe of Ephraim (Genesis 48)

Ephron: a Hittite from Hebron, from whom Abraham purchased the cave of Machpelah (Genesis 23)

Er: the son of Judah, husband of Tamar (Genesis 38:3, 6, 7; 46:12)

Esau: the son of Isaac and Rebekah, older twin brother of Jacob, ancestor of the Edomites (Genesis 25–36)

Euphrates River: a large river in western Asia (Genesis 2:14; 15:18; 31:21; 36:37)

Eve: the first woman; created by God from one of Adam's ribs; mother of Cain, Abel, and Seth (Genesis 3:20; 4:1)

Firmament: another name for heaven, separates the water above from the waters beneath (Genesis 1)

Gad: the son of Jacob and Zilpah, ancestor of the tribe of Gad (Genesis 30:11; 35:26; 46:16; 49:19)

Genealogy: a list of names that traces a family's history (Genesis 4:17-26; 5:1-32; 10:1-32; 11:10-32)

Genesis Apocryphon: one of the Dead Sea Scrolls that praises Sarah's extraordinary beauty

Gerar: a city west of the Dead Sea, one of Abraham's stopping places (Genesis 10:19; 20:1, 2; 26)

Gilead: a mountainous region east of the Jordan River (Genesis 31; 37:25)

Gilgamesh Epic: an ancient Near Eastern flood story that has many parallels to the Flood story in the Bible

Goshen: a region in northeastern Egypt where Jacob and his family settled (Genesis 46–47)

Hagar: handmaid of Sarah, mother of Ishmael (Genesis 16; 21)

Ham: the son of Noah; father of Mizraim (Egypt), Put, Cush, and Canaan (Genesis 5:32; 6:10; 7:13; 9:18, 22; 10:1, 6, 10; 14:5)

Hamor: the Hivite prince of Shechem, whose son raped Dinah (Genesis 34)

Haran: Abraham's homeland near the Euphrates River (Genesis 11:31, 32; 12:4, 5; 27:43; 28:10; 29:4)

Hebron: a city to the southwest of Jerusalem, Abraham's home in Canaan (Genesis 13:18; 23:2, 19; 3:27; 37:14)

Hittites: a people who lived in northern Canaan during the patriarchal period (Genesis 15:20; 23; 25:10; 49:32)

Hivites: Canaanite inhabitants of Shechem during the time of Jacob (Genesis 34:2; 36:2)

Horites: the Hebrew word for the Hurrian people, who were widely scattered throughout the ancient Near East (Genesis 14:6; 36:21, 29, 30)

Idumeans: the later descendants of Esau; Herod the Great was an Idumean

Intertestamental Literature: nonbiblical literature written between 200 B.C. and A.D. 100

Isaac: the son of Abraham, father of Esau and Jacob, one of the patriarchs (Genesis 21–28)

Ishmael: the son of Abraham and Hagar, who later became the father of twelve princes (Genesis 16–17; 25)

Ishmaelites: the descendants of Ishmael; Joseph's brothers sold him to a caravan of Ishmaelites on its way to Egypt (Genesis 37; 39:1)

Israel I: the new name God gave to Jacob (Genesis 32:28)

Israel II: the descendants of Jacob

Issachar: the son of Jacob and Leah, ancestor of the tribe of Issachar (Genesis 30:18; 35:23; 46:13; 49:14)

Jabbok River: an eastern branch of the Jordan River where Jacob wrestled with the angel (Genesis 32:22)

Jacob: the son of Isaac and Rebekah, younger twin of Esau, ancestor of the twelve tribes of Israel (Genesis 25–50)

Japheth: one of the three sons of Noah (Genesis 5:32; 6:10; 7:13; 9; 10)

Jared: the son of Mahalalel, grandson of Kenan, father of Enoch (Genesis 5)

Jerusalem: called Salem in Genesis, the site of Abraham's encounter with Melchizedek (Genesis 14:18)

Jordan River: the major river in Canaan, flows from the Sea of Galilee to the Dead Sea (Genesis 13:10-11; 32:10; 50:10-11)

Joseph: the son of Jacob and Rachel, father of Ephraim and Manasseh, ancestor of the tribes of Ephraim and Manasseh (Genesis 37–50)

Judah: the son of Jacob and Leah, ancestor of the tribe of Judah (Genesis 37–50)

Kenan: the son of Enosh, grandson of Seth (Genesis 5)

Kenites: a seminomadic people from the Negeb (Genesis 15:19)

Keturah: one of Abraham's wives (Genesis 25:1, 4)

King Lists: an ancient Near Eastern list of kings and how long they ruled

GLOSSARY OF TERMS

Laban: the son of Bethuel, grandson of Nahor, brother of Rebekah, uncle of Jacob (Genesis 25–31)

Lamech: the son of Methushael, father of Noah (Genesis 4–5)

Leah: daughter of Laban; older sister of Rachel; wife of Jacob; mother of Reuben, Simeon, Levi, Judah, Issachar, Zebulun, and Dinah (Genesis 29–33)

Levi: the son of Jacob and Leah, ancestor of the tribe of Levi (Genesis 29:34; 34:25, 30; 35:23; 46:11; 49:5)

Levirate Marriage: the law which says that a man must marry the widow of his dead brother (Genesis 38)

Lot: the son of Haran, grandson of Terah, lived in the Jordan Valley (Genesis 19)

Machpelah, Cave of: the burial place of Abraham, Sarah, and Jacob in the city of Hebron (Genesis 23; 25:9; 49:30; 50:13)

Mahalalel: the son of Kenan, grandson of Enosh, father of Jared (Genesis 5)

Mahanaim: a place east of the Jordan River where Jacob encountered two angels (Genesis 32:2)

Manasseh: one of Joseph's two sons, born in Egypt, ancestor of the tribe of Manasseh (Genesis 48)

Mandrake: a plant used in the ancient world to promote fertility (Genesis 30)

Melchizedek: the Canaanite king-priest of Salem who bestowed a blessing on Abraham (Genesis 14:18)

Mesopotamia (Aram Naharaim): a country between the Tigris and Euphrates Rivers (Genesis 24:10)

Methuselah: the son of Enoch, father of Lamech (Genesis 5)

Methushael: the son of Mehujael, grandson of Irad, father of Lamech (Genesis 4:18)

Midianites: a people from the desert region of Midian, probably synonymous with Ishmaelites (Genesis 37:28, 36)

Migdal Eder: a primitive structure built by shepherds somewhere near Jerusalem (Genesis 35:21)

Mizpah Benediction: a modern term for the covenant between Jacob and Laban (Genesis 31:49)

Mizraim (Egypt): the son of Ham, grandson of Noah (Genesis 10:6, 13)

Moab I: the son of Lot by one of his daughters (Genesis 19:37)

Moab II: a territory east of the Dead Sea (Genesis 36:35)

Moriah: the site in the region of Shechem where Abraham offered Isaac (Genesis 22:2)

Naphtali: the son of Jacob and Bilhah, ancestor of the tribe of Naphtali (Genesis 30:8; 35:25; 46:24; 49:21)

Negev: the desert region in the southern part of Canaan (Genesis 12:9; 13:1, 3; 20:1; 24:62)

Nephilim: the children born in the union of the sons of God and human wives; the name means "giants" (Genesis 6:4)

Nile River: the river that flows through the center of Egypt (Genesis 41)

Noah: the son of Lamech, father of Ham, Shem, and Japheth (Genesis 6–9)

Oak of Weeping: an oak tree near Bethel, under which Deborah, Rebekah's nurse, was buried (Genesis 35:8)

Onan: the son of Judah who refused to produce offspring for Tamar, his dead brother's wife (Genesis 38; 46:12)

Patriarchs: Abraham, Isaac, Jacob, and sometimes Joseph

Peniel/Penuel: an encampment east of the Jordan River, named by Jacob because there he saw God face to face (Genesis 32:30, 31)

Pharaoh: a general term for the ruler over Egypt (Genesis 37–50)

Potiphar: the captain of the pharaoh's guard and Joseph's master in Egypt (Genesis 37:36; 39:1)

Rachel: daughter of Laban, younger sister of Leah, wife of Jacob, mother of Joseph and Benjamin (Genesis 29–33)

Rainbow: the symbol of God's covenant with Noah (Genesis 9:12-17)

Rebekah: the daughter of Bethuel, sister of Laban, wife of Isaac, mother of Esau and Jacob (Genesis 24–27)

Reuben: the son of Jacob and Leah, ancestor of the tribe of Reuben (Genesis 37–50)

Salem: the earlier name for Jerusalem, where Melchizedek blessed Abraham (Genesis 14:18)

Sarah: the wife of Abraham, mother of Isaac (Genesis 17–23)

Sarai: Sarah's original name before God changed it to Sarah in Genesis 17:15 (Genesis 17–23)

Seth: the son of Adam and Eve, a replacement from God for Abel (Genesis 4–5)

Shechem: Abraham's first stopping place when he entered Canaan, an important city during the patriarchal period (Genesis 12:6; 33:18; 34-37)

Shem: the son of Noah; ancestor of the Elamites, Assyrians, and Arameans (Genesis 5:32; 6:10; 7:13; 9–11)

Sheol: the place to which the dead went at the time of death (Genesis 37:35; 42:38; 44:29, 31)

Shinar: a region that included Babylon (Babel), Erech, Akkad, and Calneh, synonymous with Babylonia (Genesis 10:10; 11:2; 14:1, 9)

Simeon: the son of Jacob and Leah, ancestor of the tribe of Simeon (Genesis 37–50)

Sodom: a city in the Jordan Valley, home of Lot; God destroyed it because of its wickedness (Genesis 13–19)

Succoth: a city east of the Jordan River where Jacob stayed for a short time (Genesis 33:17)

Syria: a country on the east coast of the Mediterranean Sea, north of Canaan

Tamar: the wife of Er; mother of Perez and Zerah by her father-in-law, Judah (Genesis 38)

Terah: the son of Nahor, father of Abraham (Genesis 11)

Terror of God: a panic that fell on the cities in the region of Jacob's journey from Shechem to Bethel (Genesis 35:5)

Threshing Floor: a place where grain was separated from straw; Jacob's family stopped at the threshing floor of Atad to mourn him (Genesis 50:10-11)

Tigris River: called Hiddekel in Genesis, a river in western Asia (Genesis 2:14)

Tithe: one-tenth of one's goods, given to God; Jacob agrees to do this if God will provide for him (Genesis 28:22)

Ur of the Chaldeans: the original home of Abraham's family (Genesis 11:28, 31; 15:7)

Utnapishtim: the hero of the Gilgamesh Epic, an ancient Near Eastern flood story that corresponds to the biblical story of Noah and the Flood

Yahweh: the Hebrew personal name for the deity

Zebulun: the son of Jacob and Leah, ancestor of the tribe of Zebulun (Genesis 30:20; 35:23; 46:14; 49:13)

Ziggurat: a kind of temple-tower found in ancient Babylon, a model for the tower of Babel (Genesis 11:1-9)

Zilpah: handmaid to Leah, mother of Gad and Asher (Genesis 29:24; 30:9-12; 35:26; 37:2; 46:18)

GLOSSARY OF TERMS   **111**

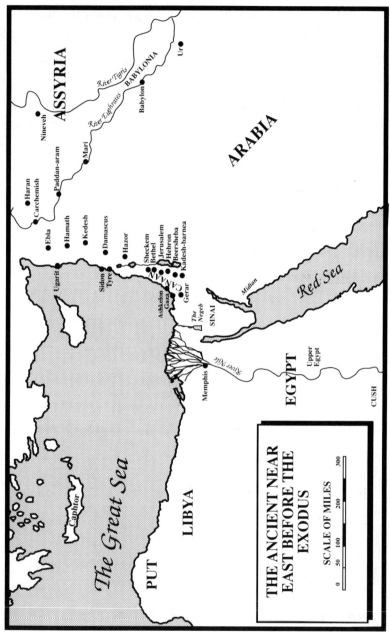

THE ANCIENT NEAR
EAST BEFORE THE
EXODUS

SCALE OF MILES

0   50   100   200   300